TANKS ACROSS THE DESERT

TANKS ACROSS THE DESERT

THE WAR DIARY OF JAKE WARDROP

EDITED BY
GEORGE FORTY

Foreword by
Major General W.M. Hutton CB, CBE, DSO, MC, MA

SUTTON PUBLISHING

First published in 1981 by William Kimber & Co. Ltd
Godolphin House, 22a Queen Anne's Gate
London, SW1H 9AE

This version published in the United Kingdom in 2003 by
Sutton Publishing Limited · Phoenix Mill
Thrupp · Stroud · Gloucestershire · GL5 2BU

British Library Cataloguing in Publication Data
A catalogue record for this book is available from the British Library.

ISBN 0-7509-3253-8

Typeset in 11.5/15pt Photina MT.
Typesetting and origination by
Sutton Publishing Limited.
Printed and bound in England by
J.H. Haynes & Co. Ltd, Sparkford.

Contents

In this diary the term 'wog' has been used by the author to describe Arab tribesmen. While we recognise that the term itself is offensive to many today, its use in the diary is very much of its time and for this reason we have decided to retain the author's usage.

Acknowledgements

I would like to thank the following for their invaluable assistance in providing me with information and photographs for this book.

Individuals: S. Beard, Esq; Andrew Biwandi, Esq; Major Dennis Cockbaine; Major and Mrs Arthur Crickmay; Major David Daniels; Colonel Paddy Doyle; Major K. Dudley; Mrs Clutha Garnett; A.E. Hall, Esq; Major General Jim Hutton; Colonel Deryck Macdonald; Mrs Enid Meehan; Brigadier E.C. Mitford; Major Dai Mitchell; Mrs H. Simpson; Eric Smith, Esq; George Stimpson, Esq; Eric Thompson, Esq; General Sir Richard Ward; Major W.C. Wood; Major Arthur Wellesley and the many members of 'B' Squadron (5RTR) Old Comrades Association whom I met at their 33rd Annual Reunion Dinner.

Establishments: British and Commonwealth Shipping Company Ltd, Photograph Department, Imperial War Museum, BBC Hulton Picture Library, RHQ Royal Tank Regiment, Tank Museum, *Tank* Magazine, BBC Radio Sheffield, Granada Publishing Ltd.

The Fighting Fifth

In the misty morning darkness, squat and ugly monsters rest
Heavy armoured, grim and deadly, with their guns all pointing west
Out behind them on the skyline, yet another morning breaks
For the past long shivering hour, every crew has been awake,
Awake and watching every movement ready for the show to start
It's the dreaded Fifth Battalion, once again they're taking part.
Swift and deadly this Battalion, pick of England's fighting chaps,
Hardy veterans of the desert, rightly named the desert rats.

As they sit there tensely waiting, silence changes into hell
And the earth is split and blasted by a hail of shot and shell,
Thick and heavy grows the barrage, till it's like a solid wall,
Flying steel, and orange flashes, shells a-shrieking as they fall.
See the cruisers gliding forward, slow at first then speeding fast,
Straight into that mad inferno, rocked and swayed by heavy blast;
On they go towards the Germans, probing, searching as they go,
Stopping now and then to batter with 6 pounder at the foe.

In and out they keep on creeping, keeping in a staggered line,
Then the air is split asunder as a cruiser hits a mine,
In the twinkling of a second all the crew are 'baling out',
They've been spotted by their comrades, watch that hornet wheel about
Back he goes just like an arrow, stops while all his pals climb on,
Such a lightning piece of action, Jerry doesn't know they've gone.
One observant German gunner tries to strafe the helpless crew
But to hit that swerving cargo is as much as he can do.

Look now, are the lads retreating? No! It's just a bit of bluff,
They're trying now to draw the Germans, so the Grants can do their
    stuff,
True enough they've fallen for it, on they come into death's jaws,
See them lurching slowly forward, twenty of them, all Mk.IVs.
Much too late they see their blunder, madly try to turn around,
But Grants and Shermans wait there ready, 75s begin to pound.
Deafening grows the noise of battle, fifteen Jerry tanks on fire,
See the others fleeing westward, smashing through their own barbed
    wire.

So once again we're moving forward, to establish our new lines,
Now we've got the job to hold it, while the engineers lay mines.
We know the Jerry panzer Div. men will not take it lying down,
And we expect at any moment an attempt to take the ground.
But the Fighting Fifth is ready, morning, noon or dead of night,
And if Jerry wants his ground back, by the gods he'll have to fight.
So off now we'll go to leaguer for a short but hard-earned rest,
And the Hun will still remember that our guns are pointing west.

This poem, written by a member of the Fifth, was presented to General Jim
Hutton when he handed over as Commanding Officer at Homs in 1943. It
was accompanied by the signatures of every NCO and soldier in the
Regiment – 420 in all, and is a cherished memento.

Foreword

MAJOR GENERAL W.M. HUTTON, CB, CBE, DSO, MC, MA

In May 1962 I wrote the foreword to Sergeant Jake Wardrop's unique diary of his experience as a member of the Fifth Tanks in the Second World War. Nineteen years later I have again been honoured by a similar request. This time, thanks to Colonel George Forty, the diary is being published in the sort of setting it so richly deserves, with comments on Jake's early life and service and the background to the many operations in which he took part. They are clearly explained in an interesting manner, with just the right amount of technical detail to aid understanding of the events covered.

Included also are many excellent photographs, which should be of great appeal to those who fought in that war and of interest to many who did not. I congratulate George Forty on his achievement, which will I hope help to enshrine the memory of Jake and the magnificent men like him.

After re-reading his diary I can do no better than repeat what I wrote as a foreword to the first privately published version, namely that as before it has left me with a feeling of deep humility.

I was always aware when commanding the Fifth in the war that the spirit of the battalion was second to none in the British Army as I knew it. Now, thirty-seven years later, I can still say this with complete certainty. This spirit stemmed from within the Fifth itself and was I sincerely believe to a very large extent due to men like Jake Wardrop and his comrades.

I felt when serving with them that it was the superb quality of the Senior NCOs which gave a very special strength. Jake, in his diary, pays a most generous tribute to the officers; in my turn I should like to pay this tribute to the NCOs and in particular to sergeants such as Jake himself, who crewed and commanded tanks for so long and with such outstanding success throughout the last war.

No words of mine can adequately express the debt which is owed to such men.

Jim Hutton
Javea (Alicante), Spain
3 May 1981

Preface

While this book is first and foremost a tribute to the actual writer of the diary, the late Sergeant Jake Wardrop, it must also be a tribute to another member of the same fine regiment, without whom the diary might never have seen the light of day. The late Major Jack Garnett MC was a corporal in 5RTR at the beginning of the Second World War, and a squadron commander with a Military Cross by the end of it. It is true to say that he, like Jake, epitomised the splendid fighting soldiers which the Royal Tank Regiment has long numbered within its ranks. And it was Jack who, knowing of the existence of the diary and the fact that it had been sent home to Jake's mother by another of his old friends, Sergeant George Stimpson (see 'The Last Battle'), made a rough copy of it when he visited Mrs Wardrop in 1958. For some time this copy lay in a tin trunk in Jack Garnett's attic, then in 1962 he decided to put it into a more presentable form. It was very much a labour of love for Jack; indeed he likened it to the self-imposed task of 'Old Mortality' in Sir Walter Scott's novel of the same name, who dedicated the latter years of his life to travelling the Scottish Lowlands, removing moss and lichen and recutting the inscriptions on the old gravestones of the Covenanter Warriors, so that the memory of their deeds should remain fresh for future generations to read. The diary, edited by Jack Garnett, was subsequently published by RAC Publications at Bovington Camp and distributed privately among the officers and soldiers of the Royal Tank Regiment. It was also serialised in the Regimental Magazine during 1976–7.

I know that every member of my regiment who has read the diary has felt that it gives a really true-to-life and graphic account of tank soldiering in the Second World War, which deserves to rank beside similar diaries from the Great War and even approaches the famous ones from the Peninsular days. I certainly felt so when, in 1974, I was researching for my very first book – about the 7th Armoured Division – and avidly seized upon the diary as a perfect source of authentic material. Jack allowed me to quote from it in my book *Desert Rats at War* and at the time I told him that I felt it deserved to be read in its entirety by a much larger audience than just the members of our regiment. Fortunately he agreed and gave me his permission to use the diary in any way I saw fit, if I could find an interested publisher. Jack had been given the permission of Jake's mother to use the diary as he wished when he first made a copy. Sadly, by the time I found a willing publisher, Jack had joined Jake in the 'Green Fields', but through the kindness of his widow, Mrs Clutha Garnett, I was able to continue with the project. Fortunately, too, I have had magnificent support from many old friends of both Jake Wardrop and Jack Garnett.

I am therefore very proud indeed to have been able to bring the diary 'into the open'. It tells of war through the eyes of one tank crewman and of the battles fought by one tank, of one squadron of one regiment. There must be thousands more like Jake, whose stories will never be told, so in a way perhaps Jake speaks for them all. I am also delighted that I was able to persuade Major General Jim Hutton to write the foreword for this book, as it was he who wrote the foreword to the original privately circulated diary and was naturally the ideal choice to write this one. I think that the love and respect which every soldier of 5th Tanks had for their Commanding Officer, 'Fearless Jim' as they called him, shines out of the pages of the diary in the same way as it has done from the many letters I have had from other members of the Fifth who served under Jim Hutton.

You may search the pages of the Order of Battle of the British Army of today and you will not find the 5th Royal Tank Regiment. The regiment was disbanded on 7 December 1969 and I attended their Disbandment Parade, which was held at Wolfenbuttel in West Germany on a rainy November day in 1969. It was a sad and moving occasion. However, the other regiments of the Royal Tank

Regiment remain to carry on the traditions, having absorbed their heritage, as we have done with all the other RTR regiments which have been disbanded in past years. We are very fortunate in being able to contract into ourselves, retaining our name, our badge and our traditions, despite such cuts. Thus it is that the spirit of such men as Jake Wardrop and Jack Garnett will live on.

A New Beginning

It is over twenty years since *Tanks Across the Desert* was first published by the now sadly defunct William Kimber & Co. Ltd of Queen Anne's Gate, London, so it has long been out of print and only available, occasionally, in second-hand military book specialists. I was, therefore, understandably delighted when Sutton Publishing Ltd, for whom I have always had the highest regard, suggested that they should produce a new edition, thus helping to keep alive the memory of Jake Wardrop and all those other gallant Royal Tank Regiment soldiers who had served in 5RTR during the Second World War.

Despite the fact that the Royal Tank Regiment has now been whittled down to just two regular regiments, the RTR Old Comrades Association still flourishes, with branches all over the UK. These include 5RTR's own special OCA, which meets once a year for an annual reunion dinner at the Victory Services Club, London. Run by their Founder President, Major Denis Cockbaine, it is still attended by a large number of those surviving into the twenty-first century. In fact, as editor of our Regimental Magazine, *Tank*, it is always a great pleasure for me to include details of their forthcoming reunions and then to follow them up with the nostalgic reports about these yearly events once they have been held.

So the memories of 5RTR live on, despite the fact that even more wartime members have now passed on to the 'Green Fields Beyond'. These include such RTR stalwarts as Major General 'Fearless Jim' Hutton CB, CBE, DSO, MC, MA, whose stirring Foreword still has its rightful place in the early pages of this book; General Sir Richard Ward GBE, KCB, CB, DSO, MC, who commanded 'A' Squadron and went on to become one of our Colonels Commandant; Major General

Rea Leakey DSO, MC*, who commanded 5RTR at the end of the war; Brigadier E.C.O. 'Long Range' Mitford MC, renowned desert explorer, who helped to form and build up the LRDG; and of course, 'Little George (Stimo)' Stimpson who was one of Jake's closest friends. The list sadly goes on and on, but despite these losses the regiment and its history remains undimmed, with new challenges to face.

Fear Naught!
George Forty
Bryantspuddle
August 2002

* I was fortunate enough to be invited to edit Rea Leakey's tremendously exciting autobiography, *Leakey's Luck – A Tank Commander with Nine Lives*, which has also been published both in hardback and paperback by Sutton Publishing.

Introduction

Jake Wardrop, The Man

Jake Wardrop, or to be strictly correct, John Richard, for that is how he was christened, was a Scot, born in Glasgow on 16 May 1918. He was known as Jack by his family; however, to prevent any confusion I shall call him by his Army nickname of 'Jake' throughout this book. There were four children, two boys and two girls, Jake being the second eldest. When I began my research I had great hopes of locating surviving members of his family, as I had their old address in Maryhill, Glasgow. Unfortunately, however, I quickly discovered that Maryhill had been extensively modernised, most of the houses and tenement blocks having been swept away and the families rehoused elsewhere.

As the weeks went by I became more and more despondent, then, quite by chance, I found out that one of the sisters had married and moved to the Sheffield area. I wrote to Sheffield newspapers, local radio and TV stations and asked them to please help me find her. *Exactly* one week before the deadline date set by my publisher to hand over the completed manuscript, I received a telephone call from Mrs Hilda Simpson, Jake's sister, who had been told of my appeal over BBC Radio Sheffield and had kindly phoned me. Thus I was able to tie up many loose ends. She explained that her brother had been a normal, fun-loving youngster, very keen on outdoor pursuits such as scouting and swimming. He and his brother also spent a lot of time canoeing on Loch Lomond. Educated at Woodside School, Kelvin Bridge, Jake found it difficult to settle to a routine nine to five job. He began training as a dental mechanic, then switched to painting and finally decided to join the Army. He had inherited a love of mechanical things from his father who was an engineer, so it was perhaps natural that he should choose tanks. In 1937, aged nineteen, he enlisted, becoming 7888470, Private Wardrop J.R., Royal Tank Corps.

Jake entered a very different Army to the one in which he would serve in wartime. These were the 'palmy' days of peacetime soldiering. Jake would have joined the RTC at the Regimental Depot, located in Bovington Camp near Wareham in Dorset. It was there that all recruits received their basic training on courses lasting about thirty-six weeks. One of Jake's contemporaries, Major Dai Mitchell, now retired, but still working as the Squadron Technical Officer of the Lulworth Support Squadron which provides the tanks and other vehicles needed to run the RAC Gunnery School at Lulworth Camp, a few miles from Bovington, explained to me:

'Our squad sergeant was a Sergeant Wilson, a great character, respected by everyone. In those days (1938) the squad sergeant was a man of many talents, guiding and teaching his way through thirty-six weeks of training. . . . The first five weeks consisted of drill and more drill, mixed with lashings of PT, and this was followed by thirteen weeks of tank driving and maintenance. We had Adjutant's drill parades twice a week of course and after eighteen weeks were given ten days' leave, the squad being marched down to Wool station all looking very smart in their new blue patrols, carrying black swagger canes with silver crested knobs. After leave we went to Lulworth for our gunnery training on medium tanks (3 pounder guns and Vickers machine guns) and Mark IVB light tanks (machine guns only). This period lasted for six weeks and was most enjoyable, Lulworth being noted for excellent 'nosh', and the weather that year was wonderful. It was a great thrill becoming a member of a tank crew for the first time. Then back to Bovington for our military education at the RTC Depot. The remaining weeks were spent putting on the final polish – pistol drill and firing, twenty-four hour guards, ceremonial drill, PT tests and passing out parades. A few fell by the wayside, squads dropping to about eighteen men, but at the end of the day the Tank Corps finished up with fully trained soldiers.'

George Stimpson joined the RTC at exactly the same time as Dai Mitchell, and together they found themselves posted to the Fifth Battalion at Perham Down, where they arrived on a wet November afternoon, with a feeling of apprehension, wondering what their reception would be like. After all the bustle and shouting of the Depot, they found the ordered tranquillity of the battalion very different. After being shown their barrack room they were taken to the cookhouse for tea, and were a little surprised to find everyone else in civilian clothes so that they, in their box-creased tunics, gleaming buttons and puttees, stood out 'like sore thumbs'. However, both remember the feeling of warmth and comradeship typified perhaps by their first meeting with Jake, as George Stimpson recalls:

'Jake was an "old soldier" with a whole year's more service than me. He had been detailed to show us our beds and take us to the dining room for a meal. During the meal we found it easy to talk to each other and immediately became friends. From this first meeting we were never far away from each other, sleeping in the same barrack room, quite often in the same tank crew, but at the same time we had lots of mutual friends and were really part of a group. At the end of each day during the war this group always tried to locate each other and to exchange a few words and cigarettes.'

Jake, George and Dai were all members of the medium tank section of C Company, 5RTC; their troop sergeant was Jock McLeod, who is also mentioned in the diary. The light tank section was under Sergeant Paddy Maloney and one can well imagine the banter and rivalry that existed between the two sections. Both McLeod and Maloney were 'built like barrack room doors' as Dai Mitchell put it, '. . . two splendid men, the salt of the earth'. The company was about sixty to seventy men strong, billeted in two barrack blocks, with the company office about fifty yards away and the tank park about 150. Reveille was at 0600 by bugle, all room jobs had to be completed by company parade at 0745, then on to the tank park by 0800. Crews worked on their vehicles until lunch at 1300, the afternoon being entirely devoted to sport in which everyone joined. A great deal of trust was placed on the individual soldier, permanent passes being issued after a year's service, which meant one could stay out until reveille, wear civilian clothes, and so on.

Sport played a very big part in most of their lives, 5RTC at the time being famous in army boxing and rugger circles. Many of those mentioned in the diary were members of the boxing team; Jake and Stanley Skeels were both middleweights, while 'Tweeny' Dai Mitchell was the regimental bantamweight. In the boxing season almost the entire day would be spent in training. Boxers need to be determined people and this certainly shows in Jake's character, for example, in the way that he continued to keep up the diary even under the most difficult conditions. As George Stimpson put it:

'The diary went with him always, including the several occasions when he had to bale out of tanks. The diary is, in fact, a tribute to his determination to complete a job once it was started; the magnitude of its achievement is more than apparent when one remembers that it covered a period of five years.'

Personal courage is also something a boxer needs and Jake 'throughout the war continually insisted on being in a tank crew in any capacity, and quite often joined another crew straight after being knocked out. His disregard for his own safety was highlighted at Syke, when 5th Tanks were approaching Bremen and the leading tank was hit by Bazooka fire, killing the commander. Jake, who was commanding the following tank, quickly dismounted and running in front of the crippled tank, turned his back on the enemy and using hand signals, guided the tank back to safety.'

'Wardrop was a very brave and intelligent person, and, as he was my tank driver in the desert and on into Italy, we had a camaraderie and mutual respect that was unusual even during those very active years. During one period of some thirty days in 1941 we were shot out of ten tanks with the loss of one or more crew members per tank. This does not include other hits such as the one he describes when the turret gun was knocked back into the tank, pinning down the turret crew. I sincerely believe I owe my survival to Wardrop's prowess and initiative.' That is how Colonel 'Paddy' Doyle DSO, MC, now retired and living in Maple Falls, Washington, USA, described Jake Wardrop to me. He went on to explain that Wardrop was very much a 'Rob Roy' with a dislike for formal discipline, so that at base camp he was always in trouble, but on the battlefield, in action, he was in his element. His great buddy, Stanley Skeels, was killed at the Salerno landing, September 1943, crushed to death between two tanks when his Landing Craft beached without warning. During leave periods in the Delta Skeels and Wardrop could: '. . . cause more trouble in five minutes than the Military Police could clear up in a month.' In consequence, Wardrop 'see-sawed' from trooper to sergeant and back again, depending on the periods when the unit visited Cairo or Alexandria. As Paddy Doyle explained: 'I had no trouble keeping him as my driver for as long as I was with the 5th Battalion. After being seriously wounded at El Alamein I spent a couple of months in India but wangled an up-grade and rejoined the regiment to go to Salerno. Dear old Wardrop was available to be my driver again. I think he was just hanging on to one of his three stripes as a lance corporal, after an extended leave period in Tripoli . . . . Wardrop was at his best in action and he was the type of Britisher that foreigners could never understand and maybe never will . . .'

In his letter to me Colonel Doyle enclosed a letter he had received from Jake Wardrop while he (Doyle) had been serving at the Armor Board at Fort Knox, Kentucky. Jake had written it from Glasgow and the letter is dated 4 February 1945, so it was written during his last leave before he was killed. It is an amusing, well-written letter in which he was able to give a little 'uncensored pukka gen' about the escapades in which he had been involved, before the regiment crossed the Dutch frontier into Germany. Towards the end of the letter he talks about the expected new offensive across the Rhine:

It will be our turn soon I hope. As long as it does not start until I get back it will be fine, I'd hate to be scotching the unit up in B Echelon as the lads tear along the autobahns. In any case we should have some fun beating sense into the heads of those misguided ones who are going to carry on a guerilla campaign.

Early War Years

'I remember little of the build-up to war that summer, but what does remain vividly in my memory is being woken up with a mug of tea on the morning that war was declared – Sunday morning and we had been out on the tiles all night! Somebody switched on the radio and that dear old fogey Neville Chamberlain was quacking away. Then the penny dropped, a state of war existed between Great Britain and Germany. Life would never be the same again. The bustle and activity started within an hour and inside a week we were under canvas at Windmill Hill.'

That was how Dai Mitchell remembered that momentous day in September 1939 when war was declared. For the Royal Armoured Corps there had been an equally momentous day earlier that year when all the Cavalry of the Line and the Royal Tank Corps had been joined together to form the Royal Armoured Corps. And because it was not considered proper to have a corps within a corps, the Royal Tank Corps became the Royal Tank Regiment. At the same time companies became squadrons, sections became troops and the word battalion was dropped. However, because of the difficult period when these changes were made, doubt still lingered on for many years and the old titles remained in use for most of the war.

The 5th had left their barracks at Perham Down so that it could house a newly formed training regiment. Windmill Hill became their temporary home for the next two months, while reservists joined to bring the unit establishment up to its full wartime strength. They still had their elderly medium and light tanks, but some new A9 and A13 Cruisers did arrive direct from Nuffields. On 29 October the 5th were put at six hours' notice to move, loading of ammunition was carried out immediately and all mobilisation equipment issued. The regiment, under the command of Lieutenant Colonel E.R. Ledward, became part of the newly formed 3rd Armoured Brigade, together with the 2nd and 3rd RTR, under Brigadier John Crocker. They moved to the St Albans area, the 2nd to Luton, the 3rd to St Albans and the 5th to Harpenden, wintering in this area, billeted in private houses. Dai Mitchell remembers that there were 'plenty of pretty girls and the black beret men were made very welcome'.

Again it was decided to move the brigade, this time to the Salisbury–Fordingbridge area. Unfortunately the billets in the town were very poor, the weather was bitter with thick snow and ice on all the roads. Eventually all were moved out of the town, mostly into a hutted camp near Harnham. Lieutenant Colonel H.E. Drew OBE MC took over command on 5 April and at the end of the month orders were received for a move to France. The 5th embarked at Southampton on 28 May, landing at Cherbourg and moving by tank train to a wooded area NE of Rouen and from there on to Abbeville. 'If the period in England prior to the move was confusing, then the next month was mind boggling . . . it was a lost cause before we landed at Cherbourg', wrote Dai Mitchell.

The intention was to cross the Somme and help ease the pressure on the BEF who were falling back towards Dunkirk, but events soon made this impossible. Jake's squadron (C) fought only one action on the SW outskirts of Abbeville, which was followed by a short lull before the retreat proper began. It was not an easy march, with refugees flooding the roads and several tanks breaking down and having to be abandoned. A composite squadron, known as Z Squadron, was formed under Major H.N. Winship, containing the remaining serviceable tanks, while the rest of the regiment moved 275 miles to Brest where they embarked on 16 June, a party staying behind to destroy all the transport. Earlier, Dai Mitchell and a companion had been sent to collect kit from RHQ – he was then SQMS's driver in C Squadron – '. . . the roads were crammed with refugees and French soldiers, so progress was slow. Roads were continually strafed and bombed and we had to bale out into the ditches.'

After one such raid they picked up some wounded French soldiers and tried unsuccessfully to get a hospital to take them. Eventually they were told by an English-speaking French officer that France had capitulated and that they would have to become POWs. 'We had news for this young man and we finally "convinced" him that closed doors or not we were going through them. Grudgingly he let us slip out and away in the darkness.' They made for Brest and after many adventures managed to get on board a ship bound for England.

Disembarking at Plymouth, they eventually finished up at Warminster, where they were given the job of writing down the names of all the soldiers of C and Z Squadrons who had been left in France. 'That was about ten o'clock, then towards midday there was a roar of engines and a clattering of tracks and in drove the squadron. We tore up the lists and threw them in the air in absolute joy!' It transpired that Z Squadron had arrived in Cherbourg on 16 June, the same evening as the rest of the 5th were leaving Brest. They had loaded their remaining tanks (four light and seven cruisers) themselves and managed to escape to England.

After concentrating at Warminster the 5th moved on to Thursley in Surrey, where they re-equipped with A10s and A13s, reorganised and started training again. 'Each squadron had its own neck of the woods, with the tanks slotted around troop areas. We slept in bell tents and bivouacs, with marquees for the stores and offices. The summer of 1940 was lovely, and life was fairly pleasant, despite the rumours of invasion. Eventually, 2RTR left us in August, bound for the Middle East, and it was obvious that, as soon as the invasion threat had faded, we would follow in their footsteps. In the meantime we courted the local girls and often watched the German bombers heading up for London.' In early October the squadron was given 72 hours' embarkation leave and started to prepare for a 'long sea voyage'. A maintenance party, including many tank drivers like Jake, took the tanks by train to Glasgow for loading on the *Clan Chattan*, while the rest of the regiment sailed on the RMV *Stirling Castle* out of Liverpool. 'The *Stirling Castle* was bliss and the convoy commander made it his headquarters. We sailed out into the river to await the other ships, and a couple of days later moved out into the open sea with a large convoy and a heavy naval escort. Later, the cargo ships from Glasgow, including the *Clan Chattan* with our tanks and comrades in arms joined the convoy as we steamed into the Atlantic . . . It would be many a long day before those that survived the desert battles would see the green fields of England.'

The Regiment and its Organisation

In order to understand just how Jake's tank fitted into the overall scheme of things it is necessary to look briefly at the way in which British armoured formations were organised in the Western Desert. Of course these organisations did vary from time to time as new tactics were evolved or new types of tanks issued. At the end of Chapter 1, Jake lists the outline composition of the 4th Armoured Brigade (8H, 3RTR, 4RTR, 3RHA and 2SG) about the time when they began to receive new American-built tanks – the Honeys and later the Grants, to replace their old cruisers. This was the era of the armoured brigade group. Each brigade contained a mixture of All Arms, including artillery and engineers, together with the necessary supporting services to enable it to be self-supporting for a limited period. It is very like the current All Arms Team concept and gave the brigadier a nicely balanced force under his immediate command. In outline the composition was: an HQ Armoured Brigade Group and HQ Squadron (including ten tanks for protection purposes): Brigade Signal Squadron (to provide the HQ with communications forward to units and rearwards to division); three armoured regiments (see below); a regiment of RHA guns (towed 25-pdrs) plus an extra battery of 37mm anti-tank guns; an LAA battery (eighteen Bofors LAA guns); a field troop of Royal Engineers; a light field ambulance RAMC; two RASC companies of trucks to carry supplies; an armoured brigade ordnance company (dealing with second line repair and recovery as REME had not yet been formed); provost unit; postal detachment; and finally, a field security sub-section (POW identification, etc). Of these elements an armoured regiment would probably get permanently under command: an infantry company; an artillery battery, complete with an anti-tank troop; an RE recce party. The remainder would be under brigade control.

The armoured regiment of those days was a mixture of light and medium tanks. RHQ comprised four Stuart (Honey) tanks, fitted with the necessary radios, etc, so that the CO could command his regiment and talk to Brigade HQ. There were three fighting squadrons, one of light tanks (SHQ of four Honeys and four troops of each four, total twenty); two of medium tanks (SHQ of three Grants and three troops each of three, total twelve per squadron). This made a total of forty-eight tanks per armoured regiment. Headquarters Squadron comprised an Intercommunication troop of eight scout cars; a Reconnaissance troop of ten scout cars; together with the necessary soft-skinned vehicles and administrative personnel to look after the immediate needs of the fighting squadrons. These were divided into forward and rear echelons, both of which were further sub-divided; the Forward Echelon into A and A1 (Forward Packet); the Rear Echelon into B and B1 (Replenishment Party). Being in one of these echelons was no 'cushy number', especially those elements which had to find the regimental leaguer during the few hours of darkness, in order to bring up supplies. Navigating in the dark, across the desert, not really knowing when one might come across an enemy leaguer instead of one's own took a great deal of skill, nerve and bravery. Each unit of course had its own regimental fitters and cooks, who were ordinary members of the unit but specially trained in the necessary skills.

Late in the Desert War, when units became re-equipped with the Sherman tank, their basic organisation was again altered. This was also due to a tactical change, as from mid-1942 the armoured division became the basic battle formation instead of the brigade group. Armoured divisions then contained one armoured brigade, one lorried infantry brigade, plus all the necessary supporting elements which were for the most part kept under divisional control rather than being permanently allocated to brigades. Armoured brigades now simply contained three armoured regiments and one special infantry battalion, known as a Motor Battalion. These infantries were experts at working closely with tanks and travelled in half-tracked vehicles. Other elements, such as gunner and sapper support, could of course be put under command as and when necessary; for example, the 5RTR Battle Drill for the period shows probable attachments as being a battery of RHA guns (eight 25-pdrs or 105 mm SP guns); a motor company; anti-tank platoon (four × 6 pdrs); section of LAA guns; section of sappers. The armoured regimental organisation now consisted of an RHQ of four Shermans, plus one AA tank; three fighting squadrons each of an SHQ (four

Shermans and one AA tank) and four troops of four Shermans each, making a total of fifty-two gun tanks and four AA tanks per armoured regiment (5RTR Battle Drill shows only three Shermans in each SHQ, making the total only forty-nine gun tanks). In HQ Squadron the Intercommunication troop was unchanged, but Recce now comprised ten carriers and six scout cars. The echelon organisation had also been varied slightly but still had the same basic job of keeping the fighting elements of the regiment supplied. A REME Light Aid Detachment was now a part of the Rear Echelon.

The lowest fighting element of an armoured regiment was, and still is, the tank troop and *not* the individual tank. Tanks must, whenever possible, fight as troops, so that they can gain mutual support and protection, while making the very best use of the basic characteristics of armour, namely the tank's fire-power, armoured protection and cross country mobility. The troop leader (normally a lieutenant or second lieutenant) would command and control his troop by radio, getting his orders over the radio in the same way from the squadron leader. Dismounted Order Groups would be held for important or complicated operations, or, for example, at night in leaguer, to plan the following day's operations. A tank commander had a great deal to do, controlling his crew (e.g. giving orders to his driver where to go, or to his gunner to engage targets), map reading, passing on information, etc. Of course the more experienced a crew became and the better they knew one another, then the simpler it was for everyone concerned. Most crewmen could do at least one other job on the tank, and the more experienced could cope with everything. Men like this, and Jake is a perfect example, could be relied upon completely in battle to use their heads and not to need constant, detailed supervision. For the most part, tanks tried to get behind cover before engaging targets – adopting hull-down positions so as to make the fullest use of natural features, such as folds in the ground, to gain extra protection. This left just the turret exposed, so the enemy had a much smaller target which was protected by the thickest part of the tank's armour. By changing position frequently (known as 'jockeying') the tank commander would further increase his changes of survival in a tank versus tank battle.

CHAPTER ONE

Arrival

Editor: The diary opens with Jake's journey out to the Middle East by ship around Africa, in late 1940. By the time that 5RTR arrived in the Western Desert and was ready for battle, Wavell's highly successful campaign against the Italians was almost completed. 2RTR, who had been in the same brigade as the 5th in the UK, but had sailed some six weeks earlier, equipped with A9, A10 and A13s, played a major part in putting the final seal upon the spectacular victory won mainly by the Desert Rats of Seventh Armoured Division. In early February 1941, as part of Combeforce, they had managed to cut across the vast uncharted wastes of central Cyrenaica and establish themselves behind the Italians, who were retreating as fast as they could, but along the much more circuitous coastal road. Combeforce set up a road-block between Beda Fomm and Sidi Saleh and forced the bulk of the Tenth Italian Army to surrender. In his history of the Royal Tank Regiment, Sir Basil Liddell-Hart described the action as 'one of the most daring ventures and breathless races in the annals of the British Army'. For the loss of 500 killed, 1,373 wounded and 55 missing, Wavell's forces had destroyed an Italian army of four corps, taking over 130,000 prisoners, 400 tanks and 1,300 guns. The victory left the British in possession of the whole of Cyrenaica, apparently poised to continue their triumphant advance into Tripolitania.

However, a new figure was about to enter the lists, and one who had already given 5RTR a lot of trouble in France in 1940. This was of course the legendary Erwin Rommel, the Desert Fox. Hitler, worried about the consequences of a complete Italian collapse in North Africa, had decided to send a small number of German troops to bolster up his flagging ally. Seven days after the Italian surrender at Beda Fomm, advance units of 5th Leichte Division began to arrive in Tripoli, to be joined shortly afterwards by 15th Panzer Division. These two units formed the basis of what was to be known in future as the *Deutsche Afrika Korps (DAK)* and their commander was Generalleutnant Erwin Rommel – a reward for his spectacular success while commanding 7 Panzer Division in France. Technically he was under command of the Italian C-in-C, Marshal Graziani, and had been instructed to plan no aggressive action, his main task being to prevent further loss of Italian territory. Needless to say, Rommel took little notice of these orders and just as soon as he had sufficient troops and tanks available, he attacked, crossing the frontier on 1 April and sending the British forces reeling back.

To be fair to the British, their strength had been considerably reduced by the need to send a force to Greece and to rest some of their most experienced troops. Besides this, their vehicles were clapped out, after a long and arduous campaign. Some of those (A10s and A13s) belonging to 5RTR, after their long march to the forward area, were using a gallon of oil a mile! The DAK cut through the British even faster than they had sliced into the Italians, forcing them back towards the Egyptian frontier. And during this spectacular advance there was Rommel, right up at the front – sometimes even ahead of his leading troops – in his light aircraft, driving his men on whenever they so much as paused for breath. By early May the Germans were triumphantly established along the Egyptian border, with the whole of Cyrenaica in their possession, apart from the stubborn garrison of Tobruk. Rommel wasted a considerable amount of time, effort and precious resources, trying to subdue this tenacious garrison, while Tobruk assumed an importance to Allied morale far greater than its actual strategic value as a useful port – although it was perhaps the only decent one between Tripoli and Alexandria.

5RTR, under the command of Lieutenant Colonel H.D. Drew DSO MC as a part of the British forces in the forward areas, was forced to withdraw in the face of the German pressure, and Jake mentions some of the hard-fought engagements along the coastal route at such places as Derna. The regiment reached Tobruk on 8 April and most of it sailed to Alexandria to refit, but one squadron, under Major E.R.S. Castle, stayed behind under the command of the 3rd Hussars. (This squadron rejoined the regiment at Sidi Bish in May.) As part of the Tobruk garrison they were under the formidable Australian General Morshead (known by his troops as 'Ming the Merciless' after a Flash Gordon movie baddie of those days).

The Aussies and other Commonwealth troops stubbornly defended Tobruk against all comers, and when an Australian newspaper published an article on the siege under the headline 'Tobruk Can Take It!', Morshead was furious. 'We're here to give it not to take it!' he stormed. And his garrison proceeded to do just that, by aggressive patrolling every night – for example, they seized an entire Italian rifle battalion one night, while a Rajput patrol, who had been accused of overegging claims of enemy killed, came back after their next patrol with a sack of thirty-two human ears as proof positive!

Eventually Rommel was forbidden to make any more costly attacks on Tobruk, or to try to advance any further into Egypt. The German High Command ordered him to sit tight and conserve his strength, as they rightly appreciated the fact that the British would attack soon. This was possibly because they had at least begun to receive worthwhile tank replacements, in the shape of lend-lease AFVs from the USA. The 'Tiger' convoy, the first to use the much shorter route through the Mediterranean, arrived at Alexandria on 1 May, with 238 new tanks. Although these were mainly only the light M3 General Stuarts, mounting a 37mm gun, they were faster, more reliable and just as well armed and armoured as the ageing British cruisers. The British liked them, and as Jake tells, quickly christened them 'Honeys'. While they were training with the new tanks an American officer and a Technical Sergeant were attached as observers.

Churchill was insistent that Wavell should immediately begin an offensive to win back Cyrenaica and relieve the gallant Tobruk garrison. This pressure, despite Wavell's unwillingness, led to the two badly conceived operations known as 'Brevity' and 'Battleaxe'.

Both contained some of the bloodiest tank battles of the Desert War and achieved very little except, perhaps, to give the Germans their own little 'Tobruk' in the shape of the spirited and gallant defence of Halfaya Pass (known as Hellfire Pass by the troops), by a small garrison under Hauptmann Wilhelm Bach, who was awarded the Knight's Cross for his valiant stand – his garrison did not finally surrender until 17 January 1942, long after the rest of the DAK had been forced to withdraw, and then it was starvation which beat them.

5RTR did not take part in either Brevity (May 1941) or Battleaxe (June 1941); instead they carried out a useful period of training as part of the reformed and newly equipped 4th Armoured Brigade, with 8th Hussars and 3RTR, the latter having recently returned from Greece. They would be used in the coming Crusader battles around Sidi Rezegh airfield, certainly the hardest fought battles of 7th Armoured Division's days in North Africa.

Sergeant Jake Wardrop

A fitting place to start this episode is with Johnny Davis on a Thursday evening, 31 October 1940. The ship was loaded, we were sailing in the morning and here we are sitting around drinking beer. Henry, Dixie, the Wildcat, and the rest. It was a fair party, especially the latter end when we knocked the licensing rules sideways by drinking and singing in the 'Bertie' (after hours). What do you think of that, Pat Dollan?

I had said 'cheerio' before, at the end of different leaves, but there was a difference that Friday morning: I was off to the war and far away too. I guessed there wasn't much chaff as we hustled through the street to the Kelvin Hall to pick up our kits. There wasn't much hanging around as we boarded at eleven and at twelve we were off 'Doon the Watter'. Roddy gave us a hail as we passed 'Brown's' and I pointed out Dumbarton Rock, the Gairloch and Loch Long to the Englishmen.[1]*

---

* Superior figures throughout the diary text refer to editorial notes which will be found on pages 145–52.

It was a smashing ship, the little *Clan Chattan*; we ate like lords: there was beer, whisky and gin on board: and the crew were great guys. Most of them were from Glasgow or Scotland somewhere, and we had some fun, especially after the first week when we got into the sunshine. At Freetown we pulled in for two days and spent them buying bananas from the boys in canoes and watching them dive for pennies which we threw into the water. They were wizards and I didn't see a single penny lost.

The time was passing: soon we would be at the Equator and it would soon be Cambrai day[2] and, what do you think, it all worked out. 20 November, Father Neptune and shades of battle for the Hindenburg Line! We had a party and the day before we built a swimming pool on deck and into this the unfortunates who had never been here before were hurled; it was great stuff. One of the seamen gunners dressed up in all the queer clothes he could find and after all the silly soldiers had been ducked, we started on the crew. The only two who got away were the Skipper and the Chief Engineer. The party was a smasher: but next morning was awful bad and the ship seemed to be standing on its head.

Just about this time, the steward started to make ice cream in the afternoon and Dixie and I started to work out a little system which we carried out until the end of the trip. Each day we bought six bottles of beer and one of the engineers put them in the cooler, then at about four Tommy, the engineer, came off duty with the beer and we sat on deck and drank them and ate our ice cream. The weather was lovely and the tan was improving daily. I sat on deck and read a lot and I also dipped in the little pool which we had made – what a life!

Durban was fine, but Nemesis was stalking near. I met Stanley; he travelled on the *Stirling Castle* and we had been apart for a month, so of course we went on the binge and what a binge it was too! We got tangled up with some sailors and what a scrap there was. The odd bottle and chair went flying, but at the end Stan and I were standing back to back unthrown. I was sore for a week, but it was quite a fight.

After Durban we sailed well out to sea and saw no land until we reached Aden, the barren rocks, then up the Red Sea to Port Suez.

The battalion disembarked here from the *Stirling Castle* and went by train to Alexandria, but we pushed on through the Suez Canal to Port Said. It is nice to have seen it and at the Bitter Lakes the Aussies were playing around in sailing dinghies – they were having fun. There was an awful lot of desert on both sides, a few camels and wogs* and that was about all. We reached Alexandria on the morning of 24 December and on Christmas Day we had a farewell party – what a night!

On Boxing Day we had shore leave and with a bunch of the engineers we went to beat up the town. The Wavell push was going well at the time and there was a mild festive air about the place, so we joined in. We did all the cabarets, the pubs, the wine shops and, I think, a cinema and spoke to some of the warriors back from the desert.

The following day we started to unload the ship and put the tanks in a workshop on the quayside. By New Year's Day we had finished and were camped at Amirya, outside the town. I had saved a bottle of rum from the ship and on Hogmanay I was on guard and we killed it as the clock was striking. It wasn't a bad camp: each morning the drivers and fitters went to the workshops to help the Ordnance chaps as they worked on the tanks. At mid-day we had two hours off and we used to nip around the town. During this time I got to know it quite well. Back at camp we had a squadron canteen selling draught beer and many a 'session' was had by all.

It was about the middle of January; we went back to our tanks and prepared for the move. On 2 February we left for Mersa Matruh on the train in a blinding sandstorm. It might be worth while to stop for a minute and look at the situation. In England there had been an armoured brigade of three battalions, the 5th, 3rd and 2nd. The 2nd had sailed six weeks before us and had taken part in the push; the 3rd and ourselves had sailed together. We were equipped with A-9s and A-13s, the better tank being the A-13, and before we moved up

---

* See page vi.

the Blue,[3] we had taken the A-13s from the 3rd and they had taken our A-9s. They stayed at Amirya and later on went to Greece.

That was the situation on 2 February 1941. The brave new brigade from England – one battalion on the train at Alexandria, one left at Amirya, with a heap of junk, and another up at Benghazi or thereabouts, having driven about a thousand miles and in need of overhaul. Well done, Churchill, or should I say the British War Office? The army that was operating on the desert then consisted of an Australian division, the 7th Armoured Division, very much worn and depleted by the push from Sidi Barrani to Benghazi, three regiments of the Royal Horse Artillery with 25-pounders, the King's Dragoon Guards, with very old armoured cars, and a few infantry regiments, Rifle Brigade, KRRCs, Cheshires, while the crack 4th Indian had been pulled back and sent to Abyssinia. The trouble in Greece and Albania was building up and there was a serious shortage of troops everywhere.

The train journey took us about two days and on detraining we drove about forty miles down the Siwa track to a place that some romancer had called 'Charing Cross'. At this place we stopped for two days, then the big trek was on. We drove in easy stages to the El Adem aerodrome, which is just to the south of Tobruk, crossing the Libyan frontier at Sidi Omar. This was my first look at any frontier, except the Scotland–England one, and I got a big kick out of it. It is a deep high wire fence and is usually referred to as 'The Wire'. The weather was good, very cold at nights and in the mornings, especially as we were heading west and the sun was behind us until mid-day, but the sky was blue and I enjoyed it. One night it did rain and we were washed right out of bed. It poured down all night long and I finally got into the tank and fell asleep in the seat, wet through. At this time I was driving a sergeant from Stoke-on-Trent, known as Stooge, a very good guy, whom I had driven in France. Then there were Derek and Claude, the operator and gunner. We reached El Adem and the whole advance went to pieces. I wondered why and can only think that the reason was the Greek war which was, by this time, the middle of February, having a growing amount of German support. The Wavell advance had stopped at about El

Agheila and, in fact, some of the troops were being recalled to the Delta – they had been on the desert since the previous summer and fought a long campaign.

The line at El Agheila was very thin and it was thought, I suppose, that the Italians were too disorganised to come again for a while, but about that time a certain gentleman arrived in Tripoli with the Afrika Korps, Erwin Rommel, the bold bad policeman. I remembered listening to a commentary about that time by Cyril Falls, on some running battles which had been fought in the Med, in which most of the Italian stuff had reached Tripoli. He suggested that those ships had German troops, how right he was! I guess Cyril knows his onions.

But we sat at El Adem and drunk Aussie beer and went to Tobruk now and again for a swim. Stanley and I did a lot of walking here, because we liked to keep on our toes and in any case we got away from the rest of them for a while. We covered miles and talked, my – didn't we talk! We organised the Army, the British government, settled the Indian problem, went to Honolulu four times and the North Pole twice; we used up some breath. It was a pleasant life: we traded tea for eggs with the wogs, played some football and I read *Gone with the Wind*. By this time we were all sunbathing.

I don't know how it started, but one day we moved and it was the slickest bit of work we ever did. For four days the battalion covered a hundred miles a day over desert that even the wogs wouldn't go on. At the end of the trip we were facing the Agheila salt flats and it was 30 March. Out of fifteen tanks in C Squadron, fifteen got there. The Major came and shook hands with all the drivers, it wasn't a bad effort. On the 31st we worked on the tanks and at night orders came round to pack up and stand by. A party of tanks of A Squadron had been fired on that afternoon by none other than the blue-eyed boys of the Afrika Korps. They had got themselves sorted out in Tripoli and come whopping down the coast and were on the other side of the salt flats. We were silly boys to be where we were! They had the 15th and 21st Panzer Divisions and 90th Light, a pretty good motorised infantry division. The British front line at that time consisted of the 5th Tanks, 3rd RHA, KDGs and the 6th RBs.

On the morning of 1 April, the fun began: a real how d'ye do it was! Stukas, Dorniers and a few thrusts by tanks. We came back that day and the next, until about four in the afternoon, when we reached Agedabia,[4] where it was decided to have a dabble. It was the quickest, deadliest duffy I've ever seen. We sat behind a ridge and waited until they came, then popped up and let loose. There seemed to be nothing in front but tanks coming on, but we kept on firing and they slowed down and finally halted and shot it out stationary. But they were feeling for the flanks and their Artillery had started to lob some 105s over. Well, there wasn't much else to it, we drew out slowly firing until it was dark. We had lost five tanks and there were casualties on several others.

That was the only serious attempt made to halt them before Tobruk that I have heard of. From then back, all the way we stayed between them and all the stuff that was going back, all the lorries and non-combatants. We had a great time with the rations, cakes, tinned milk, peaches, pineapples and as many cigarettes as we could smoke. There were dumps of sausages, tea and sugar: didn't we drink some tea! That rammy on the ridge seemed to have tamed the Bosches a bit, because we dawdled along at the rear and saw no more of them. I think we bought the dummy to a certain extent there. We headed for the coast, but it transpired that they did the same, only they made for a point further east than we did and, in fact, cut us off at Derna.

The tanks, we had six by this time, were in a shocking state and could only do ten miles an hour when we hit the main road and headed for Derna. The petrol problem was becoming serious, in the column there were two officers with scout cars and they covered miles searching for dumps by the roadside. We reached Derna, which is down on the shore situated a bit like Arrochar, only there were two 'Rest and be Thankfuls', one into the town and another out of it. At the bottom of the hill, two tanks flogged out, this was the hill going out of the town, we had managed one. Just as we were making some tea, a scout car screams up with an officer who wants to know whether the tanks have any ammo. He gets a few cracks, somebody wants to know whether he wants to buy any, but he says, 'no', that the Bosches are at the top of the hill and if we want to see our mothers again, we'll have to make a fight of it. There are four tanks and about a hundred infantrymen of the RBs, so they chased away up the hill to hold the fort and cause a shindy while we had our tea.

The plan was for the tanks to get up the hill, get into line and dash across the aerodrome, firing everything, and reach the road beyond, halt and see what developed, then let the RBs get away in their lorries. There seemed to be quite a number of faults in this. The big one being that nobody knew the Bosche strength, but I wasn't looking for an argument and, in any case, it was a 'slap-happy' effort and it was our bad luck to be here and ('hell mind you')! So off we went up the hill, the British war effort, four tanks that Caplan would not have been inclined to part with five cents for! At the top we shook out into line, the Major waved a flag and we were off. There wasn't much there, a few anti-tank guns and some spandaus, but the charge broke them. They fired some shots and broke, one tank of ours was hit and stopped. We were next to them and picked them up as they baled out and they clung to the sides. At the road we halted and the RBs dashed up the road to Tobruk – it had worked.[5] There were still ninety miles to do and at about fifty miles from home, mine and another tank flogged out. One had been losing oil for a long way and mine had been running for a long time without a dynamo chain and the batteries were so flat that they would not operate the coil ignition. There wasn't a tow rope between us, they had all been broken at previous attempts to start the tanks on different mornings. In any case, the remaining tank would not have pulled the skin off a rice pudding: so the two crocks were blown up. There were four crews to be carried and we all piled on to the last hope and off we went to Tobruk, fingers crossed.

About fifteen miles from the town our troubles ended, our nervous troubles at any rate. We crossed the defences, helped along by a loud cheer from the Aussies, who had settled down to hold the place. The tank was driven to the workshops and we lazed around for a few days, washing our kit and drinking tea. The battalion was being rounded up in little packets and after about a week, half were given rifles and put on the perimeter and the other half went to form a little tank force, so Stooge and myself took a trip to workshops for an iron monster. It was a reconditioned job and on the road I pushed her up to 42 – she was a hummer! This crowd, about twenty tanks, camped in an old ammunition dump dug under the ground. The ammo was gone and as there was a lot of bombing, this under-the-ground idea seemed a very good thing. The tanks were camouflaged and there wasn't much doing. Dusty Rhodes, a very crafty man from Birmingham, endeared himself to all by salvaging a truck one day, writing a note asking for the beer issue for the 297 Light Ack Ack Regt, signing it Major Rhodes DSO, and he got it too from the NAAFI – they were a bit bomb happy. There were a few scares and turn-outs here, but we didn't fire a shot. The Bosches attacked one or twice, but they got no change from the Aussies and they all went down to Capuzzo and sat on the wire.

On about 12 May, the party with the rifles were pulled out and set off for the harbour, the boat was in. I was told this by an eye-witness. They had jumped out of the lorries and had about four hundred yards to go when a couple of Stukas came over and bombed the ship and, cub's honour, they watched it sink. There were a few wounded, but there was another ship in a couple of days. The remaining half of us handed the tanks over and sailed on 20 May at five in the morning. I remember the time quite well because I watched a little perky lieutenant commander, the skipper of the destroyer *Defender*, as we got on board. He looked at his watch and said, 'Right, five o'clock, take her away' and the lads with the kitbags and all the junk, messing around on the quayside, had had it. That's the way they do it in the Navy.

It was a good trip, we went flat out all the way. I fell asleep on the deck and put the finishing touches to an already pretty good tan. We landed at Alexandria and by seven that night Stan and myself had borrowed a pound and were sampling the beer in Mustapha barracks canteen.

For the next three weeks we camped at Sidi Bish, which is about ten miles to the east of Alexandria on the sea front. It was a good place. The weather was lovely and I spent most of the time swimming and sunbathing, but to start off we had five days leave and what a time! There were four of us, the same four as were in the guard room at Amirya and a notable session was held in the Golden Bar.

At nine in the morning we hit the place and at five the following morning we decided to call it a day. I suppose the whole of the MEF passed through the place – Aussies, Springboks, Kiwis, soldiers and sailors, but we sat them all out. There was a band in the place and I gave the violinist a nod to play La Paloma; it's a mighty nice song that. We slowed down a bit after that except for a party in the Royal Cinema. The film was *The Thin Man* but there was a bar inside and I never got a glimpse of Myrna.

There was a general inrush of Greeks at this period as the war there had finished. I met a nice girl at Stanley Bay where I was swimming one day. We went out a few times, but the lads objected as we were strictly a staff combination: in any case the urge of John Barleycorn was working. I saw her a few times later and again the following summer when we had come back from Alamein. The troops were coming back from Crete also then and a lot of them camped beside us. There were Argylls, some county regiments, Royal Marines, Commandos and, of course, the New Zealanders. They made a great name for themselves there. The Third Tanks had arrived from Greece where they had a hectic time and took a few good beatings. Bob Crisp, the South African cricketer had got himself a DSO for a smashing rearguard in which they lost all their tanks.

Some of the Commandos were Spaniards, ones who had been fighting for the Government and had baled out to avoid prison or the wall when the war ended. They were very stout lads and had a good name among the Marines and others who had been in Crete.

At the end of three weeks, we moved to Beni Yusef, which is down by the Pyramids outside Cairo. During this time we were equipped with American light tanks which were known as 'The Honey'. They were great little tanks, fast and reliable, but the gun was just 37 mm. I did a trip to Port Said to unload some Matildas, also two or three jaunts to Tel-el-Kebir to collect tanks. There was a good canteen here and we had our share of Canadian beer. One of the waiters and I became firm friends, he was a great big Sudanese and he taught me Arabic. I gave him some shirts and socks – imagine a Sudanese wearing socks – and some tea and sugar now and again. He had a longing for my blue pullover and asked for it nightly. I persuaded a few of the lads to walk to Sakhare to the steep pyramid and some ruins. It was ten miles across the sands in the sunshine and the wogs we met on the way thought we were mad.

I did a lot of walking here around the canals, talking to the wogs and improving my Arabic. The villages were out of bounds, but I was invited to go to quite a number of them. I liked them, they are hard working people and they are exploited to an awful extent. All the summer they work in the fields and it is one long fight against the sunshine. On the outside edge of the irrigation system they have to carry water in pails and throw it over the ground so that the beans will grow, and the cotton, so that there will be a cotton crop for the financiers to buy and sell to make an honest penny.

On 15 September we entrained at Giza for the blue again. I was driving the squadron navigator, a little captain and what a good guy he was. Dixie was driving Stooge by now and there were quite a number of changes all round. The formation was the 4th Armoured Brigade – consisting of ourselves, 3rd Tanks back from Greece and equipped, and the 8th Hussars. We had the 3rd RHA with 25 pounders in the brigade, also the 2nd Battalion Scots Guards. We had trained quite a bit together around Beni Yusef and the formation was an experiment in as much as previously there had never been tanks, guns and infantry all together like this.

The commanders of units were all under orders from the brigadier of the tanks to make plans and all fight together as one. The brigadier was an old 5th Battalion man. He had been at the battle of Cambrai in 1917: he was a great guy and had a lot of desert experience.[6] The whole brigade was part of the 7th Armoured Division and the little desert rat had been painted on all the tanks. The Commander of the division was General Gott, who was killed just before Alamein. There was another armoured brigade in the division, composed of 6th Tanks, 7th Hussars and

3rd Hussars. They also had guns and infantry attached and, as well as these two brigades, there was a strong support group of guns and infantry under Brigadier Jock Campbell. There was also a couple of regiments of medium artillery to 5-inch: so you see it was quite a division.

CHAPTER TWO

Crusader

I have it in command from the King to express to all ranks of the Army and RAF in the Western Desert, and to the Mediterranean Fleet, His Majesty's confidence that they will do their duty with exemplary devotion in the supremely important battle which lies before them. For the first time British and Empire troops will meet the Germans with an ample equipment in modern weapons of all kinds. The battle itself will affect the whole course of the war. Now is the time to strike the hardest blow yet struck for final victory, home and freedom. The Desert Army may add a page to history which will rank with Blenheim and Waterloo. The eyes of all nations are upon you. All our hearts are with you. May God uphold the right!

Text of signal sent by the Prime Minister to General Auchinleck on 15 November 1941

Editor: One of the results of the failure of Brevity and Battleaxe was the replacement of Wavell as C-in-C Middle East, by General Sir Claude Auchinleck. The British and Empire troops in the desert were also grouped together to form the Eighth Army, under Lieutenant General Sir Alan Cunningham. Almost immediately Auchinleck found himself under the same Churchillian pressure to mount an attack as had bedevilled his predecessor. He resisted for as long as he could, trying to build up his strength especially in tanks. However, mere numbers were not going to be the complete answer, as the

British still had to face the unpleasant fact that German tank guns outranged their own by at least 800–1,000 yards, a significant advantage in the open desert.

The aims of the Crusader operation (Jake calls it 'the November Handicap') were to relieve Tobruk and at the same time to destroy the bulk of the enemy armour, thus forcing Rommel to withdraw from Cyrenaica. In outline Cunningham's plan envisioned Godwin-Austen's XIII Corps (2nd New Zealand and 4th Indian Divisions and 1st Army Tank Brigade) holding down the Axis forces along the line of the Egyptian frontier, whilst Norrie's XXX Corps (7th Armoured and 1st South African Divisions, 4th Armoured and 22 Guards Brigade Groups), swung in a wide left hook around the desert flank, then to drive north-west and get to grips with the enemy armour in the general area just south of Tobruk. 4th Armoured Brigade's role in the operation was, as the extreme right-hand formation of XXX Corps, to act as flank guard and maintain a link with XIII Corps. The two to one numerical advantage of British tanks over German (discounting the Italians) would, it was felt, allow them to close with the enemy and inflict massive casualties, despite the enemy's superiority in tank armament and armoured protection. The British fighting spirit would win the battle and the ringing tones of the various Orders of the Day issued before the battle reflected this optimism in such phrases as 'superior mobility', 'outmanoeuvring the enemy' and 'getting within killing range'.

The chosen battlefield was a good one for armour, vast stretches of hard gravel, with but few areas of soft sand or broken, difficult going. The climate at that time of year was bad – blisteringly hot days and bitterly cold nights. Innumerable dust-storms reduced visibility almost to zero in seconds, while sudden heavy rainstorms could quickly turn good, hard going into quagmire. Other problems which always affected mobile operations in the Western Desert included the difficulty of telling friend from foe at long range, the trials and tribulations of accurate desert navigation and the relative unreliability of radio communications. Battles themselves brought their own special hazards as well as shot and shell, in the shape of choking clouds of dust from vehicle movement, bursting shells and burning vehicles, until it often became well-nigh impossible to see through this 'fog of war'.

In telling the part played by 5RTR in the main battle Jake also mentions just one of the incidents in which the legendary Brigadier Jock Campbell, then commanding 7th Armoured Brigade Support Group, features, acts of bravery that were to win him the Victoria Cross. The 5th had been summoned, along with the rest of 4th Armoured Brigade, by the GOC 7th Armoured Division, Major General 'Strafer' Gott, in a last-ditch attempt to save the Support Group from being wiped out. Together with 7th Armoured Brigade, the Support Group had advanced northwards to Sidi Rezegh earlier in the battle, with the aim of linking up with a breakout force from Tobruk, but this did not happen. Instead, the leading regiment of 7th Armoured (6RTR) ran into heavy fire from an 88 mm detachment of von Wechmar's 3rd Recce and the guns of the Böttcher Artillery Group, and were virtually annihilated, losing over three-quarters of their tanks.

Worse was to follow. The bulk of the Afrika Korps (15th and 21st Panzer Divisions) had now turned north-west and was heading for Sidi Rezegh, with 4th and 22nd Armoured Brigades snapping at their heels, thinking that the Germans were withdrawing to avoid combat. The two remaining regiments of 7th Armoured Brigade (7H and 2RTR) had been moved to meet this new threat and suffered heavy casualties. One can well imagine the scene of carnage as 4th Armoured approached the battlefield, the opposing forces being now so mixed that it was almost impossible to tell friend from foe. The two leading regiments (3 and 5RTR) got entangled together as they swerved to avoid heavy enemy anti-tank and artillery fire, which all but slowed their counterattack to a crawl.

It was then that Jock Campbell took charge, leading the tanks into the attack in his open, unprotected staff car. His sentiments were that tanks should charge no matter the odds. Protests were met with the reply: 'That's what you are soldiers for – to die!' Indeed one officer summed up the situation very well when he said that most people were far more scared of Jock Campbell than they were of the enemy!

An RAF pilot, flying over the Sidi Rezegh battlefield, later gave the following description of the scene below him:

Guns were blazing on all sides as these land cruisers made for each other. It was impossible to pick out from our position which was which. Most of them were on the move, but there were several stationary and no longer firing. Several hundreds of them appeared engaged in a grim showdown. It was like looking down on some huge prehistoric arena with fire-breathing, scaly-sided monsters pitted against each other in a terrific struggle, lumbering slowly forward, swinging this way and that, each intent upon the destruction of the other. It must have been a concentrated hell of shell against shell and steel against steel.*

The casualties to both sides were extremely heavy, and although the Germans could be said to have won the tank battle around Sidi Rezegh, especially because their far more efficient battlefield recovery service was able to salvage their not too badly damaged tanks and get them away for repair, the eventual outcome of Crusader must be seen at least as a territorial victory for the British. XIII Corps had been steadily working around the enemy positions of the frontier and, in a bid to rescue the situation, Rommel took 15th and 21st Panzer Divisions right through the rear areas of XXX Corps and on to the frontier.

Had he succeeded in his gamble then there would have been virtually nothing stopping him from pressing on to Cairo. Certainly this view was held by Cunningham, who, completely out of touch with both his corps, was convinced that he had lost the bulk of his armour, and felt that the only answer was a complete withdrawal back to Egypt to regroup and face this new enemy threat to the Delta. Fortunately Auchinleck did not agree and personally flew up to the front to take charge, before replacing Cunningham with Major General Neil Ritchie (then Deputy Chief of Staff Cairo HQ).

* *The Second Great War* edited by Sir John Hammerton, Waverley Book Company, 1946.

But this time Rommel had overreached his lines of supply and was running short of almost everything. The elastic would stretch no further and, as neither XIII nor XXX Corps disintegrated as he had expected, he was forced to order a general withdrawal. Once they had appreciated the situation the British began a cautious advance themselves and, as Jake tells, by the end of the month they were in El Agheila, with the Afrika Korps right back where they had started so confidently nine months previously.

Sergeant Jake Wardrop

Once again we detrained at Mersa Matruh and drove to Charing Cross. In easy stages we moved across the blue, down the Siwa track and westwards towards the wire and Comrade Rommel. For about two months we waited, did some shooting and a few schemes and passed the time walking and making tea. On one of my walks across the blue I got lost and spent the night on the sand with nothing but a shirt and shorts and wasn't it cold! The following morning I hit the camp just as a search party was about to leave. There was not much said about it and in any case I comforted myself with the philosophy that I knew how hard the desert was – one false move and you've had it. The lads pulled my leg a bit, but they didn't know. I just thought, 'They've never been out of sight of the tanks, so they could not get lost.'

About 14 November we started to move into position and on the night of the 17th we were in lines ready for a march at a position ten miles this side of the wire, in line with Fort Maddalena. This was the southern prong of the drive and there were others at intervals to the north, right to the sea. That same evening the engineers went forward and pulled down a few sections of Mussolini's fence to let us through.

At 3.30 on the 18th we started up and moved forward. The November Handicap had started. That day we covered eighty miles and turned northwards to reach the coast. The garrison in Tobruk was still holding out and we had to go and let them out. Just before dark, we sighted a few Bosche armoured cars and knocked a couple out, the others got away: so the cat was out of the bag. On the 19th there were one or two little rows with Italian tanks and we took some prisoners. That night we had a scrap in the dark with some tanks. It was an inconclusive affair, there were no targets, just the flashes from the guns and the tracer shells coming and going. Ours were red and, trust the Italians, theirs were green and yellow. I'll bet Mussolini wore a green and yellow tie!

It was late when we got to bed and as the custom was, we formed up in a square, guns facing outwards, with the petrol and ammo lorries inside – just like the old covered wagon days. We adopted this formation[1] every night and the lads used to be able to drive into it in pitch darkness and half asleep. We were up before light and the order came over the air to break out a little and have breakfast – we finally got it about three that afternoon. We had just got on the move and a lot of shelling started and the reports started to come in about tanks. As soon as the fun began, we fanned right out to see what was happening. On the wireless there were ten tanks here, ten there, then someone would report another twenty-five. I was sitting in the seat hoping that they were all reporting the same ones. But no, it is an established fact that we took on the 21st Panzer Division that morning and why not, it was 20 November – Cambrai Day! 'Forward Five' and we got into line and advanced to the fray.

We held them for about an hour and during that time the 3rd Tanks and 8th Hussars were pushing in from the left and right and shooting them up from the sides. They turned and ran for it, leaving nine behind.

The great thing about this scrap was the fact that we had fought back the crack German division and they had bigger guns and thicker tanks. The losses were heavy, we had six killed in the squadron and about ten wounded, while most of the tanks had been hit and some were ready to be written off. Dixie was wounded that morning very badly, when we pulled back for ammo I saw him being taken away and he looked awful bad.

There was a quick shuffle round of crews and tanks and the ones which were fit and complete went back to wait in case they came back. So we sat for a long time and about three o'clock, as nothing had developed, we had breakfast.

Still heading north, we pushed on to get to contact again, but there was nothing more doing that day. The next morning we pushed off at first light and it was raining, but we had quite a day. Captured some field guns, lorries and a crew of motor cyclists, until at night we were involved again with some tanks just as it got dark. It had been raining all day and the ground was soft. I think we were in a bad spot, but at any rate the lorries with the petrol and ammo were all stuck and we had to carry the petrol to the tanks, about a quarter of a mile. By good luck there was a huge rum issue that day and about an hour after I'd drunk mine, I felt that I could have carried eight gallon cases of petrol until dawn.

I used to laugh when we went to bed, we had a crew bed of all the blankets laid on top of one another and the whole thing was covered with a tarpaulin. The drill for retiring was that we all removed our boots, counted from the top, one, two, three, four, five and in. In the morning we rolled it all up and tied it to the back.[2]

The next morning we started again at first light. It was Saturday and we were buzzing along steadily, passing a lot of prisoners walking back and looking sorry for themselves. About noon we stopped to eat and a message came over the wire to stand by to move – we were going to Sidi Rezegh aerodrome where there was a large-sized party going on. When we arrived there was a general state of chaos such as I've never seen before or since. There were tanks and lorries all over the place, some blazing, guns firing, and the whole place was covered with a fine cloud of dust. On the landing ground there were planes burning, and others destroyed – what a mess! Nobody seemed to have much idea of what was going on and we milled around for a bit.

Just about that time Jock Campbell arrived and took over the whole show. He came running up in a car, shouted over 'Follow me' and we chased after him for about half a mile round the airfield and there they were – a long line of Mark IIIs and 50-millimetre anti-tank guns, so we went to town on them. We pulled out to get some ammo and another squadron took over and it was decided to give them the good old charge again. Quite frankly, I was not so strong for this charging business, although we continued to do it until

about the next year at Knightsbridge, but off we went. We went
storming in right up to these tanks, firing as we went, and then
swung away a bit to go further on and beat up some artillery. There
was a terrific noise all the time, our guns and theirs and somewhere
behind they had some really big artillery which was lobbing shells
amongst us. I was beginning to think we were doing fine when a
shell burst just in front and the left track was broken, in fact we ran
right off it. What saved our bacon was the fact that it was getting
dark and everybody was passing us and the shelling was going away
from us. We sat for a minute or two, then I ventured forth to see
what damage had been done. The track was lying about twenty
yards behind and in coming off it had ripped the ration box clean off
the tank and the tins of stuff were all smashed. The cruellest blow of
all was the smashing of a bottle of whisky belonging to the
commander.

It wasn't a very healthy position to be in, but it could have been
worse: it wasn't raining. The problem was to get the tank to the
track, or vice versa and it was a heavy lump to carry unless we split
it into sections. We got in touch with the unit and told them what
had happened and the answer came back over the air to 'watch our
steps' and 'keep our chins up' and some more cheery patter!

I could hear something approaching us, in fact it had been
dinning on my ear for a bit. Far be it from me to start a panic, but
the others heard it too, so we jumped in to do battle. Anticlimax! It
was another Honey, the lame duck, one of the 3rd Tanks. We gave
him a hail and he pulled in and took us on tow, but just to tidy the
place up, we got him to reverse and pull the track behind, where we
tied it to a shackle with a piece of wire and we were off.

The time was eight-thirty, it was dark and all round there were
flares going up – it was like 5 November. Steve, the Commander,
called the CO up again and said we were on the move and would
somebody please shoot up a red Verey light. Up it went and we
headed towards it for about two miles until we struck the good old
covered wagon camp. Everybody was standing around the tanks
talking and some were filling up and getting rations. The
Commander went to report that we were in again, but he came in

about five minutes later to say that we were going out to beat up a German camp. That night about an hour before, they had captured the brigade echelon and we were the stooges who had to sort it out. Our tank was temporarily hors-de-combat, but Steve fixed that – we changed over to another one, the crew of it came on ours and we were off. All of us left one tank, there wasn't time to collect it. As a matter of fact, I didn't see the tank again until the next April when we went to look over the place and it was lying there where we had left it. The crew were captured that night. I lost all my kit, but I had worked it all out before that while there was plenty of kit about, there was only one Wardrop and it wasn't the first lot I lost, nor was it the last by a long way. I should worry! I had my toothbrush, my money, revolver and my blue pullover.

It was quite a party, the information was that the Bosche had captured this crowd of ours and had remained in the same place. The position was known – it was about five miles away – and off we went to round them up. Most of the officers had a slight binge on but for some reason there was no rum that night and the lads were all cold sober. As we approached the place, an officer of B Squadron went up to the camp just to make sure we were at the right spot – we were. He fixed a red Verey light and was hit about four times at point blank range – he and his crew baled out and got away, except the operator who must have gone the wrong way. Then the fun really started! We all cut loose at once and after about fifteen minutes we closed in and gave them the charge. A few escaped in the car, but it was a huge success. There was quite a number of prisoners, guns and tanks and a fair amount of booty like rations and bottles of lime juice. The Germans had a lot of this and, as a matter of fact, it was a thing we never had and we used to pull their legs about it and tell them we lived on salt water and sand.[3]

It was now about three in the morning and we refuelled and did a thirty mile move up towards Tobruk, then had an hour's sleep in the tanks. The attacks at the frontier had been quite successful, we were pushing out along the coast and a big crowd of Bosche had been by-passed in Capuzzo – they finally pulled out in the middle of January. The next day we reached the perimeter of the Tobruk defences and by a strange coincidence, the officer who came out to meet us in a tank was Colonel Willison, who was second in command of the 5th battalion at one time. It was quite a reunion. Later in the day there was a terrific scrap around El Adem and by night time we had been thrown out of the area and the lads in Tobruk were on their own again. At first light, we pushed in again and I think that it was just about this time that the rot set in amongst the Bosche. They pulled back to rest and the siege of Tobruk was lifted.

It was a good job something happened as we had lost a lot of tanks and crews and were right down to about twenty in the battalion. That afternoon some replacements arrived and we had a shuffle round. We were all set to go on with the chase when orders came to get the wire and get the clamps on some tanks which were heading that way. Good old Erwin had pulled one out of the bag and gone the wrong way. There was a panic amongst the echelons and stuff at the back when the Mark IIIs got in amongst them. But it was his last throw. We caught up with them and had a running scrap in which they lost six and as it got dark we closed in on them and duffed up another three. All night long, we scotched them up and they ran out of petrol and gave themselves up in the end. The situation was clearing up a bit now, there was nothing much left to do but go back and finish off the crowd who were still being tough at Sidi Rezegh – so we turned northwards again and streaked across the blue. The big experiment of guns, tanks and infantry was proving a huge success, by this time we were operating like clockwork.[4] It was good to watch the guns getting into action. They travelled about two thousand yards behind us, but up in front with the forward tanks there was an officer of the Artillery in a tank, who was in touch with the guns on the air. When we met any trouble, the CO would take a quick look at it and pass a message to the gunner officer to take it on and that was enough. The CO was then free to direct the tanks.

As soon as he got the word, the gunner sent the message to the guns to get into action and while he was working out the range the guns would be getting down the trails. He would then pass the range and direction and all the guns would put the range, 'On that' he said and one would fire a shot. The spotter up in front would watch it burst and pass back 'Down 200, left 300, fire another'. All the guns would correct and if the next one was in the area, he flashed back the word to 'let them have it' and all the guns would cut loose at once. The whole operation took about three minutes and they didn't like it at all. The 25-pounder is known as the 'daisy cutter', as it bursts along the deck. In the meantime, the tanks would be pushing round trying to get behind the enemy, in fact we became so good at it, the CO used to say 'Give them the left flank' and every tank zoomed round. At Rezegh there was a ding-dong scrap which lasted about five days, it was very tough. They had the high ground and all the advantages, but the infantry gave them the bayonet until they had had enough. The 5th South African Division fought here, also the Kiwis, it was here that the 5th Brigade fought so well there were three VCs won there.

On the collapse at Rezegh there were very few Bosche east of Tobruk and we started the chase which was to take us down the Mekili track and back to where we had been earlier in the war. This was the period at which the steeplechase really began, from now until 20 December we chased them until they were right back behind the Agheila salt flats. We ran round them, over them and underneath them. It was cold and most nights we moved sweeping across the blue to head somebody else off. On those night marches, the drivers drove half asleep and the operators slept with the phones on their ears.

At Antelat we bought a sheep and roasted it. It seemed queer to me that we bought it, when we could have had it for the taking, but we gave the wog a bag of tea and some sugar, and he kept the skin. The replenishment was a big problem, there were no cigarettes and very little water, but we always got a laugh out of something or other. Round about Mekili I had two near squeaks, and poor old Steve, the Commander, was killed. The first time it happened like this, our set had gone wonkey and as it was important for the officer to be on the air, Steve and I went on to another tank with a good set. About an hour later the tank I had been driving was hit and the driver wounded on the cheek. He has the scar now. The following day, the set on this tank went on the loose and Steve got into another tank. It was hit and he was wounded as well as the gunner and the driver. The other two went home, but poor old Steve died on the way to the dressing station.

On 19 December a whisper went round that we were being pulled out and going back to the Delta and on the 20th the advance party of the 1st Armoured Division arrived. We were all straining at the leash to get back now that it had finished and on the 23rd we set out for Cairo. The war had fizzled out a bit, there were no Bosche east of Agheila and, as far as we were concerned, they could stay there. We landed at Beni Yusef on the 30th and were on leave the following day. I went to Alexandria and visited the Golden Bar and had a couple of sessions of La Paloma, the band was still there. On 5 January we all came back and had one Christmas dinner. The Brigadier was there and he made a speech telling us how good we were, we gave him a big cheer and all proceeded to get drunk. There was a Service of Thanksgiving and Remembrance in the Cathedral and it was most impressive. All the chaps who could, came out of hospital and there were some officers too, who had been wounded. We all stood up to sing the King, and I had such a lump in my throat I nearly cried. We settled down at Beni Yusef after this to re-equip.

CHAPTER THREE

Gazala

Editor: If anyone in the Eighth Army had thought they had seen the last of the Desert Fox then they were in for a shock. However, not even the most pessimistic among them could ever have imagined that his riposte would be quite so swift in arriving. While Crusader was taking place the Royal Navy in the Mediterranean was suffering heavy losses, four of their five capital ships being put out of commission, including the Gibraltar-based aircraft carrier *Ark Royal* and the battleship *Barham*, both of which fell prey to German U-boats. This meant less danger for Axis convoys; one in December 1941 brought to Rommel, for example, fifty-five more tanks, twenty armoured cars and a large amount of fuel. So, only a brief three weeks after he had withdrawn into Tripolitania he was back, doing again to the over-extended Eighth Army what he had done to the equally over-extended British forces, ten months previously – only this time even faster!

Jake begins this section of his diary with a description of the new Grant tanks and their firepower, which certainly came as a nasty shock to Rommel, but they were not yet in sufficient numbers to make any great difference. Within three days the DAK had taken the important road junction at Msus having, for example, practically wiped out 2nd Armoured Brigade which had lost seventy tanks in the three days, 21 to 23 January. Benghazi was taken a few days later, and by 2 February the triumphant Afrika Korps had pushed their opponents back to the line Gazala–Bir Hakeim, which they had themselves abandoned two months previously. 5RTR did not take part in this opening phase of the battle, being busy drawing their new tanks. They moved up to join 4th Armoured Brigade on 20 March, leaguering at Bir Hamain. There they reorganised into one light squadron (HQ and four troops) and two medium squadrons (HQ and three troops each).

The front was stabilised along the Gazala–Bir Hakeim line for the next three months while both sides built up their strength and Rommel tried to persuade the German High Command in Berlin to attack Malta, thus to secure his lines of communication across the Mediterranean once and for all. But they took no notice and when he realised that further delay could only assist his opponents, he again resumed his offensive. Jake tells the story of Rommel's attack on the Gazala line very graphically, so there is no need for me to enlarge upon it. He makes some rude remarks about 'a silly old man from the Indian Army' who had taken command of the division when Jock Campbell was killed. He is referring to General Sir Frank Messervy who had previously been commanding the 4th Indian Division in 1941–42. Certainly Messervy knew little about tanks and suffered the indignity of literally being 'caught with his pants down' by Rommel's attack, and was captured when his Divisional HQ was overrun. However, Messervy was both brave and resourceful, and he managed to persuade his captors that he was an elderly batman rather than the Divisional commander, and later escaped, walking back to British lines and taking over command of his division again, all in the space of forty-eight hours. Despite his personal bravery, Messervy was undoubtedly largely responsible for the poor showing of his Division during Rommel's attack. Had all his tanks been positioned in their previously reconnoitred defensive positions on the left at Bir Hakeim, then they could have dealt Rommel a mortal blow. Only elements of 3RTR got there in time – thanks to the foresight of their CO, 'Pip' Roberts – and managed to inflict a fair number of casualties with their brand new Grant tanks. However, there simply were not enough tanks to hold up the DAK, the pressure on 3RTR soon becoming too great for them to bear on their own.

Perhaps the supreme example of courage was displayed by the Free French garrison at Bir Hakeim. The Gazala line comprised a long deep belt of wire and minefields, interspersed with a number of fortified localities known as 'Boxes', which were generally held at not less than brigade strength. Bir Hakeim was the vital southernmost pivot and for fourteen days and nights the garrison, under General Koenig, withstood attack after attack from both ground and air. Rommel personally tried to get them to surrender but Koenig answered him in three words: '*Allez au Diable!*' and the garrison stuck it out until, on the night of 10 June, they were successfully withdrawn. The DAK's sweep around the southern flank continued, despite this gallant defence, then turned north-east towards Tobruk, and in the area between the Sidra and Aslagh ridges fought a series of tank battles of such ferocity that the area became known as 'The Cauldron'.

Both sides suffered heavy losses but eventually the superior German firepower won the day. One of Rommel's trump cards was undoubtedly the 88 mm anti-tank gun which Jake encountered (see also chapter notes), but even their 50 mm anti-tank (5 cm Pak 38 L/60) was superior to the British who still had 2 pounders and only small numbers of the new, more powerful 6 pounder. 5RTR had quite a fight on its hands when the Gazala battle was joined. They were up against units of 21st Panzer Division (about 170 tanks in total) which they engaged for some two hours. The action continued until the evening of 2 June by which time they had knocked out twenty enemy Mark 3 and Mark 4 tanks for the loss of seven Stuarts and eleven Grants. Casualties were relatively light. Six killed, nine wounded and forty-five missing, but the killed included the Commanding Officer, Lieutenant Colonel Uniacke. He was killed while performing a very gallant act. Withdrawing in contact, his tank was badly hit and the driver was no longer able to steer it properly. In his path, Robbie Uniacke saw a British soldier, lying apparently dead, but from his turret he could not be sure. Halting the tank, despite the fact that the enemy were close on his heels, he dismounted and moved the soldier out of harm's way. Before he could remount, he was shot and killed by his pursuers. Major Castle assumed command and after the arrival of twelve new Grants on 3 June, the regiment was able to go forward the next day to relieve 3RTR near Bir El Taaleb. The fighting was so severe in the next few days that a composite 3/5RTR was formed under Major Castle, and for the next two days they fought to assist the French in Bir Hakeim. Later, when the withdrawal to El Adem began, the brigade was ordered to 'Demonstrate' in the area of the Knightsbridge box to relieve pressure on 200 Guards Brigade. Lieutenant Colonel Jim Hutton assumed command during this period as the regiment fell back to the El Alamein line.

Rommel's cup of happiness was filled to overflowing during this phase of the desert operations, when that persistent thorn in the flesh, Tobruk, surrendered on 21 June 1942. The Führer was so delighted that he made Rommel a Field Marshal. After pausing for a short time to regroup, the DAK continued to advance, driving the British back across the Egyptian frontier to the El Alamein positions (which included the Ruweisat Ridge mentioned by Jake). This was the only defensible line between the frontier and the Delta, and the British well appreciated that there could be no further withdrawal if they were to remain in North Africa. GHQ Middle East issued a special order of the day urging everyone to stand firm. It was signed personally by General Sir Harold Alexander who had just taken over from Auchinleck as C-in-C.

By this time, however, Rommel had really shot his bolt. Once again the 'elastic' supply line was stretched to breaking point and his troops were short of all kinds of supplies, especially battleworthy tanks (of the 400 he had started with at Gazala in late May there were a mere 50 left in action). Nevertheless he attacked. He was now up against the new partnership of Alexander and Montgomery, the latter having taken over as commander of the Eighth Army. Actually his appointment came about because of a tragedy which overtook General 'Strafer' Gott shortly after he had been appointed to command. Gott, a veteran desert warrior, had commanded 7th Armoured Division during Crusader and had then been promoted Commander XIII Corps. He was appointed to command the Eighth Army in August 1942 and a few days later was flying back to Cairo from the forward area, when his plane was shot down by a German fighter. He survived the crash but was killed by machine-gun fire while trying to rescue others from the wreckage. Montgomery, probably the most famous British field commander of the war, immediately took charge of the situation and ordered no withdrawal in any circumstances.

The German attack upon the Alamein line began and was centred on the ridge at Alam Halfa, where the British had dug in their tanks in accordance with Monty's orders to fight a static battle with no withdrawal. For the best part of a week Rommel threw everything he had against the British positions, then he gave up and withdrew. This rebuff was to be a watershed in the fortunes of the Afrika Korps. The next round would be fought with the odds stacked heavily against them. Having withdrawn a few miles, the DAK and their Italian allies dug in and began to prepare their own defensive positions in great depth, between the Mediterranean and the Qattara Depression. The British did not follow up, Monty sensibly deciding that he must first build up his strength. Shortly afterwards a dispirited Rommel had to report sick – for the very first time in his life – and flew home to Germany for treatment.

Sergeant Jake Wardrop

The new tanks[1] were arriving now and they were super, the finest things we had ever seen. They had a nine cylinder radial engine, were quite fast and had a crew of six, commander, gunner and operator in the top turret and driver, gunner and loader down below. The gun was a 37 millimetre and the bottom one a 75 millimetre. The brigade was made up as before – 5th Tanks, 3rd Tanks and 8th Hussars, the same gunners, but instead of the Guards we had the 1st Battalion Rifle Brigade, a company to each tank battalion.[2] They were a very salty motorised infantry unit and they stayed with us all the time, right up to Tunis, Italy and coming home. We trained a lot around the Pyramids and in between we made a film and took part in a demonstration of shooting at a range at Almaza, on the other side of Cairo. I would not have missed this for anything – all the champs were there, Majors were ten-a-penny, the American Consul had turned out, General Auchinleck and the great man Jock Campbell,[3] now a Major-General and wearing the VC. He was now Commander of the 7th Armoured Division. The targets were some old Valentines and the range was fifteen hundred yards. It was a windy day with sand blowing about, but the gunners hit them time after time.

The man who dominated the whole thing was Jock Campbell. He was big, six feet two, and what a personality. One minute he would be striding across from one tank to another with all the brigadiers trailing at the back, then he'd nip up on to the back of the tank and watch the target with his glasses. When it was hit he would clap his hands, then he'd be driving up the range in his car while the shooting was still going on. He had a long low cut down Ford and he drove it flat out all the time.

It was a great pity he was killed. I have often thought that if he'd been in command of the division in Knightsbridge, the whole show might have been different. As it was, we had a silly old man from the Indian Army who had never seen a tank and he was so slow that he was captured the first morning of the campaign – imagine a General being captured! On the way home from the ranges when the shoot was over we met another VC, General Freyberg, of the Kiwis, he was passing in his car and stopped us. He is a great guy, too. I have seen him since in the New Zealand Club in Cairo, he and his wife went there often to see the lads.

On 16 March we entrained again at Giza for the blue, the railway had been pushed into Libya by now and the rail-head was at Gambut. The war had come back a bit, in January there had been a strong push by the Bosche, but they had been held at Gazala and had a line running from the coast south into the blue for quite a long way, where it tapered off into just a patrol area. They had minefields and strong points, as had our troops facing them. The southern end of our line was Bir Hakeim, a piece of high ground with a well on it and held by the Free French under a very tough gent called General Koenig. Up in the north there was the 50th Division all Tynesiders and a South African Division. The 4th Indian Division had come back from Abyssinia and was in the blue. There was the 1st Armoured Division, 7th Armoured Division and a lot of other tank formations and infantry outfits. It seemed to me that there was just about enough stuff on the blue to lick them, but I don't know, we never seemed to get going. Of course, a poor General makes a lot of difference. We had one ourselves until he got his 'bowler hat' and I've a shrewd suspicion he wasn't the only one. The lads fought that summer – didn't they fight! – but it seemed to get us nowhere. We were never licked; we knew that we had chased them once and we could do it again. We trained a bit on the way, too much I thought. When the balloon went up on 27 May most of the tanks had done about eight hundred miles on exercises and it was too much – after a thousand they begin to get sluggish.

As the summer wore on it got hotter and hotter, we were, as usual, well down in the desert, our spiritual home, and it was thought there wouldn't be a push that summer. We used to get some beer, American tinned, and by buying up the tins from the non-drinkers, Stan, George and I had a few mild sessions. At odd times, too, we'd get a bottle of whisky from one of the officers and that would be a big night. During the end of April and the beginning of May there is a hot wind blows up from the Sahara, it is called the *Khamseen*[4] and blows for fifty days and nights – the word is Arabic for fifty. We were camped a few miles to the east of Bir Hakeim and it was very hot indeed. Stanley and I had worked out a theory about the sun, roughly that you had to stay on your feet, if you lay down in the afternoon it had licked you: so we covered ourselves with gun oil and went walking. We used to sit and talk a lot and watch for fires at the other tanks and sidle across and say, 'Oh, you're making tea'. The water was very scarce, so was tea and sugar, but we managed. I sat all day in the sun and made a sundial on the ground out of little twigs and small shells. It was accurate for about a week then as the sun was going south to Capricorn it was out and it got worse. I often wondered how the sundials in the parks work, perhaps it has something to do with the angle the points make to the face. We used to gaze at the stars a lot and became quite good at telling the time by the Plough.

On the morning of 27 May, we were wakened at four o'clock and told to pack up and get ready to move, the party had started. We were ready in about five minutes flat and then we just sat around and had breakfast. I should say that at this time I had been driving the squadron leader, but he had gone to Cairo to give some instruction on the Grant to another crowd who were being equipped. He got back four days later, but to begin with I drove another officer – more of him later. At about ten o'clock, we moved to a position already decided on to wait for the bad men. When they arrived we gave them a good warning with the big 75. It quite shook them I'm sure and they turned and ran for it.[5] They didn't come back; so we moved to another place, gave them a good doing over, then the order came to get up to El Adem aerodrome and cut off a column which was heading for Tobruk. The day ended with a scrap at night and there were a lot of fires all over the place, lorries and tanks blazing. We camped on the aerodrome and there was a little bit of bombing during the night.

The next morning we milled around in the same area and in fact worked a bit farther to the east; there were a few scraps but nothing conclusive although it seemed that things were going well enough. We collected some boodle around here from the dumps which had been left, tins of stuff to eat and cigarettes. The next morning we worked west again towards the Bosche minefields. The news was that they had all been pushed back behind them again and that was fair enough. On that first morning quite a number of the lads had been captured and some were trickling back now. When we pulled out to do battle, a column had come round and beat up the echelon; they had been captured and set free several times as the scrap went back and forwards, but it all finished square – we lost nobody.

On the afternoon of the 29th, we were bombed as we moved along, there were quite a number wounded and poor old Pave was killed. That night we put in an attack on some anti-tank guns just as it got dark, it was a savage effort. We shelled them well from about two thousand yards then closed in for the kill. Maybe it was darkness that spoiled the shooting, or these might have been extra tough kiddies, but as we closed in they bobbed up and started lacing us with eighty-eights. The 88mm[6] is an all-purpose gun about the same size as our 3.7 AA; it fires high explosive, solid shot and anti-aircraft shells and is very bad business. I was closed down, but looking through the periscope and I saw the greeny-white tracer of one coming straight for us. I thought to myself, 'That's ours' and there was a thump on the front, then another and bump again on the front and then he didn't fire again. I was just thinking how good of him it was and what was going to happen next, when I looked back into the turret and there was nobody there. I poked the gunner in the ribs and asked him what the hell he thought of that; so I gave the loader a shout to get into the seat while I slid up into the top turret and looked out of the cupola.

There was quite a shindy going on, two of our tanks were blazing on the right and I thought that maybe we should pull back a bit and find the other three who had baled out. The loader was in the seat and I gave him the word to pull her back, but the shots from their gun had hit the sprocket and broken the track. The tank on the left was still firing, it was about a hundred yards away, so I told the two in the tank to hold the fort and dashed across to get a tow. It was Cliff's tank, and he pulled in front of us and took the tank on tow. The show was just about over by this time and we camped about a mile further back. We had taken quite a beating, three of the tanks had blazed and there were a lot of the lads wounded and burned. I went to see Snowy in the ambulance. Poor old Snowy was hit badly. I forgot to mention the brave little officer who arrived when we got on tow. He said to me, 'I thought we were on fire; did you not hear me give the order to bale out?' I just spat on the ground at his feet and walked away: if there had been nobody there I would have punched his nose.

The next morning we took our kit from the tank and went on to an ammo lorry and travelled on it all day. We went westwards again, past the scene of the tow the night before: there were quite a lot of stiffs lying around and some guns and lorries, so the shooting couldn't have been so bad after all. That night, just as we were pulling in to get down to bed, we were bombed. It was very grim, two or three lorries were hit and some of the guns. Two of our lads were killed and a lot of the gunners. One of our crew was wounded, he baled off the lorry when it started and he must have run the wrong way.

The following morning, all the crews who had lost their tanks were called together and we set off for some more to a place near Tobruk. There were plenty of them there and we loaded them on to transporters – this was my first jaunt on one, they had just come from America and good jobs they are. There was a dust-storm blowing and it held us up for a day, but we finally got going and when we were near enough to the battle area they dumped us down and went back. It was a stupid effort really, because the officer in charge of the expedition didn't know where the battalion was at this time. To make things worse, the officer was getting nervous and I didn't like it at all. We camped for the night and set off in the morning and by good luck ran across Div Headquarters. They put us on to the battalion, and about three in the afternoon we found them. It was grim. They had been in a scrap the night before and taken an awful beating. The CO (Lieutenant Colonel Robbie Uniacke) had been killed, we'd lost about ten tanks and Wag Fry, Topper and a lot more were gone. Stan and I had been together, so we went to look for George. Poor wee George had baled out and lost all his kit and he had a shrapnel splinter in his wrist. I was glad to see him.

That day we got organised into crews and I started to drive the Major again, he had been in that duffy the night before and had been on fire. The second-in-command took over the battalion and we had about twenty tanks on the road. That afternoon late, we moved up the line and took a position over. The Bosche were not far away and we had to keep an eye on them. All night we stood-to on guard and in the morning, as nothing had happened, we made some tea at the back of the tank. It was decided now that we should put in an attack, the time fixed was five o'clock and we sat in the tank and slept. I wrote my diary up to date, slept now and again, then got out and lay under the tank and thought a lot. It had been quite a war so far, it had only been on a week and it looked like going on for plenty more. I thought of a few places that I'd rather have been at that moment. Dow's perhaps, or Driver's maybe, or just Maryhill Road sitting around in my pyjamas drinking tea. I got up and had a wash, shave, cleaned my teeth and slicked my hair up – one of the crew had some hair oil. We had a lot of coloured flags on the tank and wore them as scarves, it made quite a sporty effort. They all washed after that, in fact it used to be a ritual with us to get 'queened up' a bit as though we were going to the Plaza when we had a date with Erwin.

At five to five, I started up and right on the nail we moved forward. It was a very short engagement, I think they pulled our legs a bit and we just walked in like a lot of idiots. There were a lot of tanks down behind the ridge and guns, and when we got nearer, they started to give us a pasting. Two tanks went up straight away and the crews were running for it. We picked up a few of them and were hit ourselves, but not very badly. They didn't all get back – the two commanders were missing. We fired some more and then withdrew, it had been a miserable failure.

The next day we got mixed up with some crowd with Valentines, the 44th I think. One brigade was in a pretty poor state. The 3rd Tanks had taken a few good beatings, as had the 8th Hussars. For about a week we pushed here and there all up and down the minefield, but it seemed to me that if they had got a lot of kit together and had one big push in one place, we could have done something definite. As it was, the units were just battering themselves to pieces in a lot of little scraps which were getting us nowhere.

The French at Bir Hakeim were having a pretty thin time and one night we were told that we were going to give them a hand. They had beaten off repeated attacks and the Bosche were giving them a going over with Stukas and big artillery. In the morning we went off and it was so misty that we had to halt and have breakfast – one of the few mornings we had it before twelve o'clock. Then it cleared and we carried on and got to a position near, where we sat on a ridge for the afternoon. There were a couple of Bosche half-tracks towing guns and we knocked them out and when it got dark we pulled back and camped – the big show was fixed for the morning.

Before light we rose and moved forward to the fray. It didn't come off, in fact it was another fiasco. It was like this. We were tearing in quite fast, there seemed to be nothing much about and we halted to let the Commander have a look. He spoke down the mike to me and said, 'There is a gun firing at us, but he is not doing very well'.

About a minute after that there was a thud on the front just above my head and a commotion in the top turret. I looked round and there was the 37 gun lying on the floor of the turret. The Commander yelled down to 'take it away' and I was off. It was a good tank and steered nicely, I had got it the day after that five o'clock duffy as we had been hit on two of the bogeys. I spun her round and was in top gear doing peak revs in about one and a half minutes. The Major had been hit on the knee slightly, so had the operator, and the gunner was pinned in his seat – the gun hadn't fallen on him, just alongside him and he couldn't move. We were all right down below.

As soon as we were safely out of range, we halted and got the gunner out. He was suffering from shock and had a few scratches. The major got on his dingo and went on down to another tank and the gunner was evacuated. I hung around at the back with the tank all day and there was a lot of shelling and messing around; but they didn't get to the Frenchmen.

That night, infantry of ours fought their way in with the bayonet and they evacuated the place. So ended Bir Hakeim, the desert stronghold – it was a pity. It was known that we would be needed no longer down here, not that we had done much, and that night we moved in the dark about twenty miles to the north. The Major came back on the tank and we started out. On this night trip we travelled in three columns with the navigator leading the middle one. The Major sat in front on the mudguard for a while passing lighted cigarettes through the visor now and again, then he went into the turret and fell asleep. They all did and I drove along singing to myself. It was a lovely night, the moon had come up and I was feeling good. I liked those night moves, there was something about sneaking across the desert in the moonlight that appealed to me. When we had halted and formed up for the night, I wakened the others up. The Major had a bottle of whisky and we killed it and I took a nip to Stanley, who was on another tank then.

The next morning I set off with the operator to take the tank to workshops at Tobruk, the Major took over another tank and the remainder of the crew went on the echelon. About this time the

Bosche came out again and when I arrived at Tobruk, the workshops had moved: so I drove down the track to the east to find them. This was really the last throw, this was the push that sent us back to Alamein. It took a day or two to find a place to get rid of the tank, but having handed it over I met a chap I knew with a big Scammell. He was going back to the unit, so I jumped on. We did not have far to go back, as the bale-out had started and I joined the echelon at Gambut. The tanks were a bit further west and they had been in a terrific scrap the night before. Stanley and George were still battling and I jumped a petrol lorry going up. They were in good spirits and I got back on to another tank. We had a big rum issue that night and everybody was in great form. The Bosche didn't come again, in fact they had turned back and captured Tobruk – we heard it later.

In the morning we handed the tanks over and went down the line to be equipped again and get organised a bit. The trip back took about five days and we landed at Amirya. The push had started and the news was bad. They had crossed the frontier and were coming down the coast. I don't know much about it because I wasn't there, but it must have been grim. By the time the Alamein line had been reached we were equipped and back in the field ready for more. At Amirya we had a few good jugs, there was a big canteen there and the three of us nipped into Alexandria to see if the Golden Bar was still there – it was and so was the band. The Australians were back – they had been up in Syria – and it was good to see them. I liked the Diggers, they are fighting fools. We went down to the southern edge of the line amongst the sand dunes and beat off some attacks, about two a day for four days. When there was an attack in the north or the centre, we would tear up to lend a hand, then back to the south again. They were being held and now we started to counter-attack them to pull their legs a bit. We did a few of these and although we never got far, they had the right effect. The Air Force was getting bigger, too, and we used to see the Bostons going over eighteen at a time, to warm their pants a bit. On 15 July we did an attack with the Kiwis and I had another close one.

We were scrapping against some tanks and we were hit twice on the front. I saw the sparks fly from the first one just like welding and the next line took the visor away. It is about a foot square and I lay flat and kept my head out of the way. Didn't it look a big hole though. The Major shouted down was I all right and to keep my head out of sight as he couldn't pull back just yet. I said I was doing fine thanks, but not to make a night of it. Soon after they broke and ran for it and I turned round and went back to find the fitters. They fixed the visor and I joined in again at night. It was a lucky tank that one: it was donked time and time again, but it never went on fire. As a matter of fact, when I handed it over it had been hit fifteen times and it sure looked as if it had been around. The line was holding fine and we moved to the centre to a place called Ruweisat Ridge, which was being held by the Indians, Rajputs they were. There was a minefield running between two high points and we used to camp on one side of it each night then drive through about four in the morning and string out across the valley facing west.

We did this for about a week and Stukas came three times a day, in fact the place became known as Stuka Valley. Just about this time we had a new CO Lieutenant Colonel Hutton, known to one and all as Fearless Jim. He was young for a CO, about thirty; he had the MC and Bar. He had been wounded twice and he must have been one of the greatest guys who ever joined the army. He was always well up in his tank giving orders on the wireless in a nice pleasant voice, just like the announcer reading the news. The lads would have done anything for him and gone anywhere with him – if he had said we were going to make a frontal attack on the gates of hell, they would have been off like a shot.

It was always rough in this area, there was shelling more or less all day and, of course, the Stukas. We had a direct hit on the front of the tank one day from a high explosive. It did no damage, but blew all the water tins off and knocked some chips out of the barrel of the gun and broke all the periscopes.

One night we beat off an attack by tanks. What a party! There were about thirty of them coming down the valley, but we shook them. Fearless was talking on the air, 'Here they come, Five, hold your fire a bit longer. Now, let them have it. That's the stuff.' We certainly shook them up, we knocked out fifteen. There was one flying a big blue flag and Fearless gave the order, 'Let's see you get him with the flag.' He was hit about ten times and went up in flames; it was a great scrap.

Little George had a bad one here with the bombing. His tank had been hit once and he had driven down to the fitters wagon. They came over again and he nipped into the tank; the commander and two of the crew were killed and two fitters. We carried on like that all through the summer, moving up and down the line scrapping all over the place. They were bad days, we lost a lot of good lads and didn't seem to get much for it: and yet I suppose we were doing well enough. At any rate, they had not reached Cairo yet. It was about this time John Irvine was wounded; a bit earlier maybe, about 8 or 9 July. Poor John! He was such a good lad.

Towards the end of August it was thought that a big push was developing down in the south at a place called Himeimat. So we moved down that way. The idea was, when the push came to let them through, then chop them up. The CO went out in his car and found a good position to fight from and it was settled that we'd go there when the fun started. Two or three times we practised going there and on the morning of 1 September, we had the order to move to the appointed position. We got there about four in the morning, our favourite time. All that day there was nothing doing, but towards night we could see tanks coming from the west. I was driving a second lieutenant called Dolly Grey at this time, the Major had taken over as second-in-command of the battalion. He was a good lad, but he worried too much. It was his first time and he wanted to make such a good show of it. The other two tanks in the troop were commanded by Henry Hall and a countryman called Campbell, who used to be a poacher in Perthshire. We had some Americans in the unit and this was their first blood. Late that night our troops moved round to the left and we lined up across the end of a wadi. That move round finished us, Dolly was getting too excited, so Stanley took the valve out of the set when he wasn't looking and told him the set was duff. Dolly was sure he had to have a wireless set: so he moved on to the next tank and Jock Campbell came on to ours. Stan put the valve back and we settled down for the night. I felt better after that.

We were standing-to in the turret all night. It was my turn on and I was sitting watching and listening. Was I surprised when someone opened fire on us from in front. It was dark and I could see nothing. The shots were high and too far right to do any harm, so we sat tight and minded our own business. Some time in the morning very early, I was dozing in the seat, when there was such a commotion in the turret. I could hear Jack saying to Stanley, 'Take a look at these Stan', then the answer came back, '. . . Hell'.

It was just breaking light and there in front of us, about two thousand yards away, was a great heap of tanks. They must have halted there the night before and were shaking out. I wakened the gunner and we started to go to town on them with the 75: we couldn't miss them, they were so bunched up. It was all right while it lasted, but they started to give us a lacing in return – it was quite a morning. We were hit a few times and I started up to see if we could get to a little bump and get behind it, but no, there was another bigger thump on the front – we'd had it, the track was broken. I couldn't resist saying, 'I told you so' to Jock. By this time I was an authority on tracks and the breaking of them.

Jock rang up and told the squadron leader what had happened and the reply came back to shoot it out as long as possible, then bale out. I shouted back to George, 'How many is there?', and he grinned back and reached for his haversack and revolver. I got my own stuff, put on my revolver and blue pullover and picked up my small kit – I was jumping again. About five minutes later Jock yelled down, 'Bale out' and we were off.

As we ran I looked across at Henry on the left, his head was sticking out of the turret and I waved to them and started lifting my feet. We got over a little ridge and lay down for a while, then walked across to the gunners who were belting away great stuff. We got some tea from one lot and hung around for an hour or two. The shindy was dying down a bit; in fact we were giving a work-out. They carried on eastwards and every time they tried to head north there was something waiting.

At the end of about three days they started to draw back to the west and every available plane pasted them the whole way. There were Bostons, scores of them, and the Spits were strafing the lorries and having great fun. We went back to the tank and it hadn't burned, although it had been hit a lot more. It was recovered and we went back that night to the echelon. So ended the back-to-back phase.

General Montgomery had arrived and he said that we'd start now. There was tons of stuff coming to the country, the Highland Division had arrived, and the plans were being made for the big push. There is one more thing: the following night we were in Alexandria again; we had set out to get another tank and had gone back and further back until we reached Mustapha Barracks. It wasn't very late and we dashed around and got some pay and hit the spots. Just on principle we checked up on the Golden Bar – it was still there. I got Georgie, the Greek, to play La Paloma again and I wouldn't have changed places with anybody. The morning before we had been in the blue fighting and here we were in the flesh pots, it was good. But everything has an end and the next morning we set out to get back to Amirya and picked up a tank on the way. The next afternoon we rejoined the unit and made a real big brew of tea and thought it over – it had been a hectic few days.

CHAPTER FOUR

El Alamein

Editor: The battle of Alam Halfa was undoubtedly the turning point of the desert war and the first in the long series of defeats that culminated in the eventual downfall of Nazi Germany. However, when it had been won, there was a great deal to be done before the final battle of El Alamein could be fought and we could assume the offensive. As soon as Rommel's Afrika Korps had been repulsed Alexander and Montgomery began to prepare. Monty was of course the ideal person to revitalise the spirits of the tired Eighth Army. They had stood and fought with their backs against the wall, now it was their turn to go forward. In his memoirs Monty explains how it was necessary to make everyone realise that future battles had to be fought to a definite Army plan and that a firm grip had to be kept on the battle at all times by his Army HQ, as he puts it: '. . . This led to a recognition among officers and men of the necessity for one guiding mind which would control their destinies and after this battle [Alam Halfa] they accepted me as that one mind.' This is how, with basically the same troops as had been defeated at Gazala, he was able to achieve success, and it can be summed up in the one word 'generalship'.

First of all Montgomery had to get himself known by every man in his Army and he did so, as Jake explains, by visiting every unit in the desert. Monty had an instinctive flair for publicity which he exploited to the full, and it is very appropriate that one of the major factors which he says became in the end: '. . . the means by which I came to be recognised throughout the desert' was a Royal Tank Regiment Other Ranks black beret which he wore, complete with RTR capbadge alongside his General's badge. In his great victory at Alamein the RTR would play a larger role than in any other battle of the entire war. To men like Jake it was a great tribute and pleasure to see this unconventional senior officer wearing a tankman's headgear, although at the time it must have caused a good number of senior eyebrows to be raised!

Montgomery and Alexander felt it was essential to train and equip the Eighth Army properly for the coming battle, so they successfully parried attempts by Churchill to attack too soon, spending nearly two months building up their strength. This included obtaining over 250 new Sherman tanks, mounting a 75 mm gun which was not only superior in performance to the one on the Grant, but was also mounted in an all round traversing turret instead of being stuck in a side sponson. This enabled the tank to make much better use of the ground, being able to take up proper hulldown positions and not having to expose vulnerable hull and tracks to enemy fire.

Although the Axis forces (Panzer Armee Afrika) did have the advantage of being in a strong defensive position eight kilometres deep and with over five million mines sown in 'Rommel's Devil's Gardens' to protect them, the comparative strengths of the opposing forces show a very heavy bias in favour of the Eighth Army, viz:

	Eighth Army	Panzer Armee
men	195,000	104,000
infantry battalions	85	71
medium tanks	1,029	496 (of which only 211 were German)
field artillery pieces	908	500
anti-tank guns	1,451	850
petrol	unlimited	11 days supply
ammunition	unlimited	9 days supply

Add to this the fact that the Germans and Italians were at the end of a very stretched supply line – it took a resupply convoy a fortnight to complete the round trip from the main base at Tripoli, while the British were but a few miles from the Delta. The British also had air superiority, another telling advantage.

On Friday 23 October 1942, the battle of El Alamein opened. The artillery barrage which preceded the initial attacks began at 2140 hours, with all the British artillery blasting away at the enemy, in what one German soldier who faced it described to me simply as 'The Inferno'. When the battle started Monty was asleep in his caravan, knowing that there was nothing he could do at that precise moment, but would probably '. . . be needed later' as he put it in his memoirs.

Jake, with the rest of 7th Armoured Division, had been initially placed opposite the southern end of the enemy line, tasked to carry out a diversionary attack, while the major thrust actually took place much nearer the coast to the north. This deception plan had been successful and had resulted in Rommel locating two of his armoured divisions opposite (21st Panzer and the Ariete), but when he moved 21st Panzer north to join 15th Panzer, Montgomery moved the Desert Rats north as well, initially as Army reserve. Once the breakthrough had been achieved they would become the spearhead of X Corps – the *Corps de Chasse* as Jake calls them – despite his earlier misgivings that they would be thought too cunning with not enough dash to be included! X Corps had been so badly mangled that they could not have managed the job without 7th Armoured. When one considers that most of the Division's tanks were high mileage and many were due for major overhaul, then it says a tremendous amount for the skill and devotion to duty of the tank crews and of the fitters who supported them so magnificently.

The advance now followed the well-trodden paths across Cyrenaica, the division reaching Tobruk on 12 November, Benghazi on the 19th, Agedabia on the 23rd and Agheila, on the frontier of Tripolitania, by mid-December. But do not get the idea that this advance was easy: the Afrika Korps fought every inch of the way, grimly defending every position and never letting the withdrawal become a rout. They inflicted casualties on the advancing columns as Jake explains, and received plenty themselves which they could not so easily absorb as the well-supplied Eighth Army.

Three months to the day, in the early hours of 23 January 1943, the Desert Rats reached Tripoli; first into the city were armoured cars of the 11th Hussars (The Cherry Pickers) who had been the first unit into action against the Italians on the night of 11 June 1940 at the very beginning of the war in the desert. The 11th were closely followed into the town by 5RTR tanks. Not long after the city's capture, the Prime Minister visited the victorious troops on 3 and 4 February, and took the salute at the Tripoli Victory parade. In his address he said: '. . . Ever since your victory at Alamein you have nightly pitched your moving tents a day's march nearer home. In the days to come when people ask what did you do in the Second World War, it will be enough to say: I marched with the Eighth Army.'

Sergeant Jake Wardrop

It was now about 8 September 1942, the last throw of the dice had failed and we settled down to get ready for the big push. The divisions were grouped into formations, there were three corps in the Eighth Army, and General Montgomery visited every unit on the desert. About this time a big decision was taken which is worthy of note. The 5th Battalion had been on the desert since March and it was thought that they might be sick of it, so one day a parade was called and Fearless put it to us. He gave us the choice of going to Cairo and missing the push or staying on the blue and taking part in it.

At the end of his speech he asked us to step forward if we wanted to stay and the whole battalion took a pace forward. There was no turning back then. It was a great outfit, every one of them had been in the push since it started and were prepared to go on again. We had good officers, of course, the very best and we respected them as fighting men. Every one of the majors had been in through the summer. Fearless had been in the 3rd Tanks and had been wounded at Knightsbridge and was back for more and everybody was raring to go.

The new American tanks were arriving now, the Shermans, but we didn't get them. It was thought that we would be too cunning and not show enough dash and a corps was formed – 10th Corps –

the *Corps de Chasse* – they were going to chase all the way to Tripoli. It was now that we had an infantry brigade in the division, the 131st, consisting of the 1/5, 1/6 and 1/7 Battalions of the Queen's. They went all the way and, in fact, came home with us from Italy – great men, the Queen's. All the RHA gunners were taken away to form the *Corps de Chasse* and we had a regiment from Kent. Until now we had been the 4th Armoured Brigade, but there was some change and we became the 22nd, consisting of 5th Tanks, 1st Tanks and 4th City of London Yeomanry: we still had the RBs.[1]

When Monty left England he had a few lessons to learn and one of them was given to him by the 5th Battalion. Since we had been on the blue we had used the 'one frequency' system on the air – that is, every tank was on the same frequency, also the gunners, infantry and the replenishment packet. In England they were using a frequency for each squadron and each squadron had a link to the CO – a very long-winded business. We had such good wireless discipline that everybody could pass their messages, there was no jamming, and if a tank about a mile in front was being fired on, the whole battalion knew about it.

Well, Monty didn't believe it: so one day we did a stunt for him to show how easy it was. Some derelict tanks were pulled out and we were to drive along and have a battle, as if it was real. A tent was pitched, there was a wireless set in it and a speaker, the set was on the battalion frequency, Monty was in the tent and all of his staff, the corps commanders and quite a boiling of big shots. We carried out the stunt; it was a piece of cake really. Fearless came up on the air clear as a bell with his orders, the gunners got into action and the whole thing was a howling success. There was a pamphlet printed soon after cancelling all others about wireless discipline and the standing training is now the 'one frequency' system[2] – good old Fearless!

We trained a lot at this period for the big push, stunts like going through a gap in a minefield and fanning out on the other side. The time passed and on 22 October we had a lecture from Fearless and he told us all about the coming show. He did not say when it was – as a matter of fact it started the following night – but it sounded good. The 7th Armoured Division were going in right down in the south – there were three minefields to cross and these were going to be looked after by a crowd of very tough babies who were equipped with tanks which had big rollers on the front. These rolled ahead and exploded the mines, a very good idea too.[3] On the 23rd the moon was full – the old Montgomery moon – and we shuffled around into position a few miles to the east of the first minefield. The big show was about to begin.

The line-up on the other side was quite impressive: they had two Panzer Divisions, a number of Italian Armoured Divisions, five or six Italian Infantry Divisions and such old Bosche veterans as the 164th, 90th Light and some old hand gunners. It is a joke in one outfit that when the war is over we shall send an invitation to the 90th Light to come and have a party in Tripoli – they had been on the blue nearly as long as ourselves and were quite old friends. In the meantime, though, we were out to fix them as they had been in our hair long enough. I think we had the edge on them for equipment, we had more artillery and reserves behind and the RAF were all over them.

By about 9 p.m. on the 23rd, everybody had closed right up to the minefields. At ten the barrage opened up all along the line. There were infantry attacks in many places and the tanks were to push through about four in the morning to reach the other side just as the light was breaking. Stanley, George and I were on the same tank now, the Major's, and we had a bottle of Gilbey's Spey Royal that night to keep out the cold. None of us slept, we were all a bit excited. About four in the morning we pushed off and got through the three minefields with little trouble. There was some shooting back and forwards and a couple of tanks were on fire, but we had to carry on until the open ground was reached. We had been travelling in line one behind the other, but when we reached the open ground we opened out into a semi-circle and pushed as far as possible. There was a slight hitch as another minefield was encountered, some of our tanks went up on it and they were told to sit tight and shoot it out for a bit at any rate. To our front there was some high ground with guns on it and as day broke they could see us and started to give us a lacing with everything they had. On the left there was a hill, Himeimat, and this was being taken by the Free French, the Legionnaires, from Bir Hakeim. There were a lot of air-bursts and they are bad medicine. They don't explode on impact, but with a time fuse while in the air. For instance, firing at a target three thousand yards away, the fuse is set to go off a split second before and the shell bursts in the air just overhead and the stuff comes down. It was one of these that got Paddy the Major. He was looking out of the turret, there was a loud bang outside and he dropped into the turret bleeding all over the place. We patched him up and stopped the bleeding, but there was no room in the turret to lay him down. There was no medical officer handy and there was so much shelling outside we didn't know what to do.

I pulled the tank to a slit trench and Stan and me bundled him out and laid him down, but he started to come round and wanted to get back in the tank. I went across to the KRR major, who was sitting by an armoured car making tea of all things, and asked him if he had an MO handy. He said he hadn't and suggested that we take the tank and the Major right out of the way and back through the minefields. He was a very cool specimen and I noticed he had the MC and bar, two Indian medals and the Palestine medal. He was lounging against the armoured car as though he was in Dow's getting a couple of brandies. I often wondered who he was. We put Paddy back in the tank, rang up on the air to say what had happened and started off back. On the other side we found the unit medical officer and put the Major in the ambulance. He had about four hundred State Express 555, and a bottle of Johnny Walker – so we shared them between us to pay for our trouble. In any case, I didn't think Paddy would be doing much smoking or drinking for a while. He didn't join us until next summer, after Tunis.[4]

There was a shortage of tank commanders at this time, so we went back with a man short. Stewart, the operator, did commander and operator. That day the infantry pushed in through the mines, beat up some guns and came back with a lot of prisoners. At night we were counter-attacked, but beat them off and spent the night in the tank standing to, screwed right up to high pitch. The next day was the same again, but the Queen's got dug in and some guns moved through. The whole front was the same for those first few days, there was not a great amount of progress but the Bosches had to split up to meet all the thrusts. That night, we pulled back and went up to the north where the big drive was developing. For another day we sat behind and in the late afternoon we dashed through the gap. The Highland Division had gone right through and there was a brigade of tanks in front of us having a terrific scrap right at that time. I watched the Australians as we drove through and didn't they look tough, most of them had on only boots and shorts, a rifle and bayonet and a tin hat. They were dirty and unshaven, but at that minute I wouldn't have said 'boo' to the smallest one I could see. The Highlanders took a licking here, they were lying about all over the place. I saw a piper who had been killed as he went forward blowing his bagpipes. We got to the scrap as quickly as possible, but it was just about over and although this other crowd of ours, the 9th Brigade, took a severe hiding, the Bosches had taken one too. There were Mark IIIs and IVs all over the place. That night we made as much ground as possible and camped ready for the chase in the morning.

The line had been broken well and truly and we were behind it on the blue with plenty of guns and tanks further to the west but we were off at first light and tore straight through them and off. The bugle had blown and we couldn't stop! There were thousands and thousands of prisoners. If we happened to stop beside any, we nipped out, pinched their watches, binoculars or anything they had and carried on. And then it started to rain – and didn't it pour down for about four days. We fought in the mud, got stuck in it, swore, drank rum and chased. It was around this time that we just missed catching Rommel. It was a pouring wet afternoon and someone spotted a column away to our right going in the same direction. They had a lot of our stuff, 25-pounders and Ford lorries and there was a bit of doubt as to whether they were our own, so we held our fire. Our tanks were not very fast, they were the same ones as we'd had all summer and the replacements had been overhauled and nobody could get close enough to see definitely. It was funny, they hadn't opened fire on us, but neither had anyone come across to say who they were. We were speeding up and they were gaining and pulling away. Old Fearless must have had an idea there was something fishy about it as he gave the order to halt and open fire. The range was about three thousand, visibility was poor with the rain and they were moving fast, so I guess the bad policeman got away. An intelligence report a few days later said that Rommel's headquarters had baled out of Fuka on a certain date heading west across the blue. It was a strong fast column made up of British kit and American Honey tanks. It was the same date, place and, I'm sure, the same column.

We listened to the BBC at nights on the tank radio and the news was great, most of the stuff in the line had been beaten up, the Italians and the Germans were captured in thousands. There was a push going along the coast and down into the desert an armoured division was keeping up the chase. At this bit we'd jab one another in the ribs and say, 'That's us'.

We crossed the wire about Sherferzan and turned north to Capuzzo – it was here that I took my hat off to a certain Bosche train driver; old Casey Jones had nothing on this lad. There was a little diesel engine standing on the line and as we approached he nipped out of his hut, disconnected the trucks and smoked away to the west with a burst on the whistle. I think he was giving us the Heidelberg raspberry, but good luck to him.

The push on the coast had also reached the frontier and they had captured Bardia and pushed on to Tobruk. We milled around for a bit then swooped on El Adem aerodrome and captured twenty-five Me 109s and all the Luftwaffe personnel. They were having their dinner and came rushing out of the buildings. We dropped a 75 or two amongst them and the others put their hands up. There were not many of them to put up their hands really, because that 75 is deadly stuff and in any case, the lads were fighting mad and, who knows, some of them might have dropped a bomb on the Clyde some time – it would do them good. We piled into the Mess and ate their dinner, so it didn't go to waste. You should have seen all the dirty 'desert rats' sitting round a table with a white cloth on, shouting 'Hoch' to each other – it was one of the high spots of the war.

The chase went round the coast near Derna, Cyrene and eventually Benghazi but we stayed at El Adem for two days. On the second day we had a lecture from Fearless. He told us how pleased he was at our performance and said that the Royals were keeping contact round the coast. About an hour later a heap of transporters came into the camp and there was such a shindy. There were Shermans on board and in about an hour, or less, we had sorted out a composite squadron and we were on the move across the blue. You should have seen it, there were chaps rushing about with their bed rolls, slinging them on and jumping on board.

It was the old cut off movement again. We had to get to the coast south of Benghazi to catch them coming down. We had one squadron from the 5th Tanks under the man who took over when Paddy was wounded, Major Maunsell, I was driving him. There were two squadrons from the 1st Tanks, the RBs and the 5th RHA. It was a 7th Armoured Division side and was commanded by Lieutenant Colonel Mitford, 'Long Range' Mitford, a cousin or brother of Unity, and well known desert traveller. I had spoken to him in the summer of '41, when I tried to join the Long Range Desert Group. He was a Major in that outfit then and it was said of him that if he dropped his hat in the middle of the blue he could go back a year later and pick it up.

The first day the transporters got stuck in the sand, so we sent them all home and drove it. On the third day we passed Msus aerodrome and so good was the timing that the transport planes were landing with supplies at the same time. It was round about this area that the push had always faded out and I wondered how Monty would do it. It was nearly a thousand miles from Alexandria to Agheila and in the two previous pushes the administration broke down. There was no stuff to carry on with and there had been a counter-attack. The fact that we were there with fifty almost new tanks was a change, and there were more. The Highland Division had rested and were on the way with the New Zealanders, the Scots Greys, 2nd Armoured Brigade and guns of all sizes to crack the line at Agheila. After Msus we reached Fort Antelat and cut the road to the west. There was not much stuff to capture coming from

Benghazi, as the Royals got there so quickly round the coast that they just laid down their arms.

About ten miles to the south was the village of Agedabia, where we had our first scrap in April 1941, and we captured it the next day without loss. We took the airfield and a thousand prisoners. There was only one more place before Agheila, Mersa Brega, and we encircled it and had some fun shooting up lorries on the road as they tried to bale out. At the end they put the white flag up and we drove in. On 6 December, the Scots Greys arrived and we handed the tanks over to them. Strangely enough, the lad who took mine came from Knightswood and knew Hugh Pose's shop well. We piled on to lorries and drove back nearly to Tobruk to a place called Morasses. All the stuff was arriving as we left, the line was smashed on 12 December and plans were made for Tripoli. We thought we'd miss it, but we didn't, we were back at Marble Arch[5] on Christmas Eve. It seemed silly taking us on a three-day lorry trip, but I suppose the idea was to get everything off the roads and out of the way to let those who were going to scrap get on with it.

At Morasses we had some battle dress issued. We had been wearing shorts in all that rain and cold and did a lot of eating and sleeping. At this place we had an early Christmas Dinner and had a quick refit, and on 18 December we hit the road again on transporters. I enjoyed those trips, sitting on top of the tank and nipping off for a brew every time there was a puncture. They were great guys those transporter men. They went day and night and I don't remember seeing one in an accident. At Marble Arch we got off and they drove straight back for another crowd. We had another Christmas Dinner on Christmas Day and three bottles of beer. I managed to raise a bottle of Cyprus wine from somewhere. We sat in the tank that night and drank and talked.

Boxing Day was a parade and we went over to see what Fearless had to say. He read us a message from General Montgomery to the Divisional Commander – it had been passed down to the units to be read out. It said 'You have set an example of how the battle of pursuit should be fought that will stand for all time' and a lot more, it was good. The only two places to be captured now were Sirte and Nufilia,

then there was a long way to go, a few more small places, then
Tripoli. The last two places were taken about 12 January and on the
17th we moved into position for the drive on Tripoli. From here it was
just two hundred miles and the units taking part were the Highland
Division on the coast, the 7th Armoured Division inland, and another
Division made up of the 8th Armoured Brigade and the New
Zealanders. There were plenty of guns and armoured cars and
another tank battalion on the road with the Highlanders, they had
Valentines. The 7th Armoured was still made up as before – 22nd
Armoured Brigade, Queen's Infantry Brigade (131) – and to make
things better, the 11th Hussars came back and we had the 5th RHA
with 25-pounders. The RBs were with us again, I should say still, and
the Division stayed like this from this time until we came home.

On 18 January we got out and it was a bit of duff. The first day we
didn't see an angry man and the second day we did not bump into
any trouble until about mid-day – mines and anti-tank guns. The
Highlanders were going great guns on the road and we were getting
along fine. The next day we crossed the Wadi Zem-Zem, a rocky,
steep gully which ran north-east and south-west for miles. This
would have been a good place for a hold up. As a matter of fact, the
Kiwis had had a big scrap there the previous day and we drove on.
The country was becoming very rough, hilly with steep crevices
which, in places, we could not cross. There were some houses
around here, Italian colonists, but most of them had baled out. They
were nice places made of dried mud with mud dykes around the
fields. I thought of the Mexican adobe houses down on the Rio
Grande, they are the same I would think. There were trees, too, olive
groves and green fields – it was good after the desert. That same day
the Highlanders took Misurata, which is on the coast about one
hundred and twenty miles from Tripoli. On the 21st we sent some
reconnaissance parties out to find a good path through the rough
going, but they could make nothing of it, so we turned and drove to
the coast road. At every possible place the road was blown up and
there was the odd gun to hold up the advance. We rolled them up
and made quite good time, camping a few miles west of Homs –
seventy miles to go.

At first light we cracked off and gave some help to the Seaforths as they went in with the bayonet on some high ground just off the road. It was downwards after that – we had been going up for a few miles – and the road was blown up in a few places. The Engineers got going and we drove on. It was like this until we got to within thirty miles, where there were some anti-tank ditches and two or three 88s on the other side. On the right of the road there was a drop into the sea and on the left thick woods, but we got about three tanks up and they got busy with their guns. At the same time the RBs got off their lorries and crossed the ditch further up. They closed in with the tommy gun and the pineapple, in fact they got into action so quickly that they were astride the road to the west of the guns before the crews realised it and a few more squareheads 'bit the dust'.

It was dark by now and we all baled off the tank with axes and shovels to fill in the ditch. Fearless was there with a shovel, working like a hero. It took us about an hour as we had to wait while the Engineers swept round a bit for mines. They are good lads these mine lifters and are right on the job under fire and all. They have a detector on their back, or one had, and he sweeps with a metal rod over the ground like a carpet sweeper. When it passes over metal there is a whistle in the earphones he is wearing and another one digs it out. Sometimes it is just an old bully beef tin, but they don't miss many mines. We did a night move and got to within ten miles of the town and pulled off the road.

At dawn on the 23rd the Gordons drove into the town sitting on the Valentines which had operated with them since the beginning of the push. There was a bit of doubt about who was there first; the 11th Hussars claimed it, but we were all there together. I spoke to some Kiwis and they had moved that same night to quite close to the city. It was only left then for somebody to go through the gates and it happened to be the Gordons and good luck to them – they don't come better.

We got organised a bit now and settled down to rest and sit around making tea. There was quite a lot of loot in Tripoli, rations and Army kit. We did quite well for sugar, tins of butter and things like that. There was wine and brandy too, and we did a little drinking. On the road near the camp there was a post office run by an Italian lady, I got to know her quite well. She had a coffee grinder and got the wogs to grind coffee beans for us. I gave her sugar and soap, tins of bully and stuff like that. She was a nice lady, the senora, and I felt sorry for her. It was a long way from Italy and she had had no news from home now that we had taken Tripoli. She had a smashing house, just like the old Southern homesteads on the films, with a lot of wogs to do the work, but she worried a lot about her two sons in the army. Near her lived another Italian from the Isle of Capri called Pasquale, who had some good brandy. We became firm friends, I have to go to Capri and look him up when the war is over.

On 4 February we got some new kit to wear and drove down to Tripoli for a big parade. It is a good town for shows like that, with nice broad streets and white buildings. The weather is always good, too. We got lined up facing the saluting base and went back to camp. Early next morning we went back into town all spruced up with our belts and holsters scrubbed clean, we were then told that the Prime Minister was coming.

He arrived about eleven with a great escort of motor cyclists and 11th Hussars in armoured cars. Well done the 'Cherry Pickers'; they would have to be in front! There were three car-loads of big shots, Monty, Alexander, General Leese, Randolph Churchill, Air Marshal Tedder and a lot more. They drove round the streets, past all the lads, then came back to the saluting base. Mr Churchill then met all the unit commanders. I saw him have a good long chat with Fearless, I wonder what he had to say?

Next came the Highlanders with the bagpipes and all, it was great. The Highland Divisional Commander, General Wimberley, was there, a big raw-boned Scotsman. There was a piper in the Gordons with a big black beard, if it had only been red, he would have been Rob Roy to the life! When it was all over, they all got into the cars and we cheered them down the road, then started up and drove home. It had been quite a day.

CHAPTER FIVE

The End in Africa

Editor: While Rommel's Panzer Armee Afrika was fighting its stubborn delaying action through the deserts of Cyrenaica and Tripolitania, a fresh enemy had appeared behind them in the shape of the Allied 'Torch' landings on the coast of Algeria and Morocco. There were three task forces, totalling some 107,000 troops, under the overall command of General Eisenhower. They were scheduled to land on 8 November in three main areas: the eastern task force was largely British and had Algiers as its objective; in the centre, an American force was aimed at Oran; while in the west the third task force, under the command of General George S. Patton, had the job of occupying French Morocco. The eastern task force got ashore without much difficulty, but the French forces in Oran and Morocco, still under the command of Vichy France, resisted, and fighting did take place. They did not finally surrender until 10 and 11 November respectively.

The political situation between the Allies and the French on the one hand, and between the Germans and the French on the other, was highly confused at this time, and resulted in Hitler losing patience and ordering his troops to take over. Ten German divisions marched into Vichy France on the night 10/11 November, while an ad hoc Axis force landed by sea and air in Tunisia. This force, under the command of General Walther Nehring, a former Afrika Korps commander who had been wounded at Alam Halfa, had the task of forming a secure bridgehead around Tunis and Bizerta. By the end of November there would be over 15,000 German troops in Tunisia, with tank support which included a battalion of the latest Tiger tanks (see chapter notes) which Jake mentions.

Initial contact between these forces and the Torch Eastern task force came between 17 and 23 November when the British First Army pushed towards Tunis. Their attacks were badly coordinated, lacked air support, and made little progress. By the time that they were ready to try again in early December, the complete Fifth German Panzer Armee had arrived, and although it did not contain as many troops as Hitler had promised (due to reverses in Russia), the experienced German soldiers under Generaloberst Jurgen von Arnim were more than a match for their 'green' opponents. They repulsed the Allied drives on Tunis, then took the initiative and pushed them back into the mountains, inflicting heavy casualties.

On the other front Rommel's forces had by now been pushed back to the Mareth Line, a good defensive position which Rommel was confident of holding. He therefore persuaded von Arnim to mount a counter-offensive in the north, to push the Allies back from the mountain gateways into Tunisia, while he switched the bulk of his own armour from the Mareth Line to combine with von Arnim's armour in an all-out thrust against the American II Corps in southern Tunisia, in order to clear his rear of enemy. Kasserine Pass was but one of the areas in which savage fighting subsequently took place, the inexperienced Americans suffering very heavy casualties; 1st US Armored Division for example, who were caught in an ambush, lost over 100 tanks. For some days the situation was very serious, but the German attacks were not fully exploited and all were finally repulsed with the passes still intact.

In the meantime, acting on a request from Eisenhower to relieve the pressure on his forces in Tunisia, Montgomery had been building up attacks on the Mareth Line. Rommel decided to launch a massive attack himself in the Medenine area, in early March, with the aim of halting further Allied probes. Jake tells of this battle which was in some ways similar to the one in which 1st US Armored Division had suffered so badly, only this time it was the Germans who were on the receiving end. The main attack of 15th Panzer Division came against the three Queen's battalions of 131st Brigade, who were well dug in with supporting artillery and anti-tank weapons. Brilliant shooting by the anti-tank guns of 1/7 Queen's alone accounted for 27 of the 57 German tanks knocked out. The artillery, anti-tank guns and infantry were so successful that only one squadron of British tanks was used in the battle and then only to thicken up on one position.

Not long after this disastrous battle, a tired and ill Rommel flew back to Germany on sick leave. He also went to beg the Führer to rescue his gallant Afrika Korps so that they could live to fight again in the defence of southern Europe. But Hitler refused. 'He [Hitler] seemed very upset and depressed about the Stalingrad disaster. . . . He was unreceptive to my arguments and seemed to pass them all off with the idea that I had become a pessimist. . . . It simply never occurred to him that things could go wrong in Tunisia.' So wrote Rommel in his diary. Hitler also forbade Rommel to return to Africa.

After the Mareth Line battle, the DAK managed to disengage and withdrew northwards, so that by mid-April they were holding a tight perimeter around the coastal plain in the Tunis–Bizerta area. But the end was inevitable and final surrender came a few weeks later in May 1943, over 250,000 men and masses of equipment falling into Allied hands. Just before midnight on 12 May 1943 the DAK sent off the following signal:

Ammunition shot off. Arms and equipment destroyed. In accordance with orders received the Afrika Korps has fought itself to the condition where it can fight no more. The German Afrika Korps must rise again. Heia Safari! Cramer, General Commanding.

About the same time a signal was being sent to Churchill by Alexander which read:

Sir, it is my duty to report that the Tunisian campaign is over. All enemy resistance has ceased. We are masters of the North African shores.

It was a signal which Churchill had waited for a long time to receive.

For the triumphant Allies came all the delights of liberating the city of Tunis. The leading elements of the 7th Armoured Division were first into the town, reaching there on 7 May 1943. 5th Tanks were well to the fore: indeed, it is a toss-up as to who actually reached Tunis first between the tanks of 5RTR and the armoured cars of the 11th Hussars and the Derbyshire Yeomanry. Thus ended a 2,000 mile chase which had begun six months earlier at El Alamein, and throughout almost the entire period Jake and his crew had been in continuous action.

Sergeant Jake Wardrop

While we had been sitting around Tripoli, the pursuit had been kept up by the 8th Armoured Brigade, a very salty crowd made up of the 3rd Tanks, Staffordshire Yeomanry and Notts Yeomanry.

They had chased right along the coast and were at that time approaching Ben Gardane which was one of the outposts of the Mareth Line. There were a few strongly held places around here, Medenine was one and Foum Tatahonine another. On 20 February we got on transporters and drove to Zuara, where we got off and headed south into the blue. It was quite good country on the coast, but as we got further south the cultivation thinned out, then stopped altogether – we were home again on the sand. For a few days we hung around then started to move west in very easy stages until we crossed the Tunisian frontier. The news came in one day that Ben Gardane had been captured and that we had to go and beat up Medenine.

The whole key to the Mareth Line was a ridge which lay a few miles to the west of it. If the Bosches were on it they could watch the east and the preparations for the attack, so we had to shift them off it. The attack started from a point about four miles in front of the ridge and the night before we were thirty miles from it and moved up in the dark. There was no smoking that night and before first light we had started up and moved forward. The opposition was not very strong, I think the Bosches were a bit jittery at this time, at any rate we pulled it off and even threw in a right flank which consisted of a few tanks. They sat round and across the road and when the Bosches turned to run, they let them have it. We took quite a lot of stuff here, mortars, guns and a good number of prisoners. It was a very stout performance and it was thought very well of by Monty. The ridge is now known as '5th Tanks Ridge'.

The line was pretty thin here and a few days later the Highland Division moved up and a lot of Artillery, also the 201st Guards Brigade. Further north, in Tunis, the Yanks were getting the run-around at Kasserine Pass and were withdrawing, but when the threat developed to the Mareth Line a lot of Bosches stuff came down south to throw us out. On 6 March the attack came in, but we were all ready.

The 131st Brigade had towed their 6-pounders[1] from Alamein and never used them, but they had a party that day. The 17-pounder, too, was beginning to arrive; in fact the Guards had some this day. It is a great long thing and very accurate, what a gun – one shot at a tank is all it needs. We also had medium Artillery, 4.5s and 5.5s and everybody was dug in. Just the Scotsmen and the Englishmen lying in a little hole smoking Vs and waiting. It was a great scrap, they lost sixty tanks; the sixty positives were flamers or tracks off and were left behind and the infantry attacks were all broken up. They lost thousands, the shells were bursting amongst them and the machine guns were chopping them off at the knees. On the 7th they gave the idea up and retired behind the Mareth Line to wait for us. The preparations were made for cracking the line, patrols were sent out just to keep an eye on things, and everybody took it easy for a while. I went to Djerba Island from here to see the place, it was very nice and I bought some fish to take back, but that is another story.

There were a lot of French people here, refugees from France and Syria, also a big number of Jews. They were all pleased to see us and had been having a fairly thin time lately. Back at the camp, beside one tank there was a well and the next day we were frying the fish when one of the lads passed. He asked where the fish had come from and I said, 'Out of the well'. About ten minutes later he was sitting on the edge of the well with a length of string and a bent pin with a worm on it and it wasn't even 1 April.

Stanley, George and I had not been together for a while, I was driving the Major, Stanley was operating in Jumbo Hill's tank and

George was doing the same on 12 Troop Commander. We always said that we were split up to strengthen the squadron. It made no difference really, we saw as much of each other as usual and it was nice to visit one another at times and see how we were all keeping. We played some football here and saw two films at a mobile cinema, one was Dorothy Lamour and the other was *Desert Victory*. There was an *Egyptian Mail* about in which Paddy had been given the DSO, that made him quite a big shot – DSO and MC.

The Indians had come up, also the 50th Division, the roughnecks from the Tyneside, and there was a lot of Free French, the crowd from Bir Hakeim and General Leclerc's outfit from the Chad. There was some very hard cases in this lot, real lean dry desert men. Before the big push went in there were some hills to be cleaned up and this was done by the Gurkhas and Sikhs very efficiently in a short time. The attack began on 21 March and it was a very tricky business.

Running from the coast inland south-west there was a deep wet ditch, the Wadi Zem-Zem, and it was thought that the Shermans could not get across until some work had been done to make a way over. This was impossible, as the place was under fire from the other side. However, big bundles of sticks[2] were tied up and laid handy and these were to be thrown in and the Valentines of the 40th Tanks were to try to cross. If they got on all right and made a bridgehead, the path could be laid down and we could cross, also the guns. On the morning of the 21st Infantry of the 50th Division crossed the wadi and got to work, the Valentines got over and we moved close to be ready to nip over. The show seemed to be going well enough and we sat tight all that day and the next. But the 50th were being counter-attacked and having a rough time and late at night on the 22nd we moved right up to the edge of the ditch.

As daylight broke on the 23rd, we could see right over to the other side and took on some guns and tanks. The 50th had come back during the night and were dug in around us. But Monty had been thinking too. Several days before a force made up of the New Zealand Division and the 1st Armoured Division moved to the western side of Gabes and put the lot in the bag. They had a terrific scrap at El Hama on the 23rd and the whole day in the same spot under very heavy shell fire and made the acquaintance of the 'Moaning Minnie'[3] – a six-barrelled mortar. It is built like a great big revolver with six chambers and fires six shells one after another very quickly. They sail through the air very slowly with a siren wail and very deadly, as the shells all land in the same area. It was first made by the Russians and nicknamed 'Stalin's Piano' and a very nasty piece of work it is. A salvo dropped on top of a Sherman of ours that day, killed the driver and set the tank on fire. They were landing on the guns and generally doing quite a lot of damage.

We were fairly safe in the tanks, but the Infantry had a rough time. I saw some DLIs get up and start to run back; there was one of them walking and saying, 'Don't run away'. I wonder who it was, he was a good lad. They came back and got into the trench again. That night we stood by in the tanks and the Highland Division went in, that was the finish. Next morning there were no Germans east of the Gabes Gap, except stiffs and prisoners.

I almost forgot, my commander was wounded in the hand that afternoon and was evacuated. This was the second major I'd seen in the ambulance and strangely enough, it wasn't the last. The second-in-command came on the tank then, big Ted Whitty. He was a good guy and such an aristocrat. His home is in Somerset and he had some class. He had played rugby for Bristol and cricket for Worcestershire, been all round the world and knew everybody.

Very much later on, when the scrapping was finished, the Divisional Commander visited us. He said 'Good morning' to the CO, then went up to Ted and shook his hand. This was a general speaking to a major, he was a big shot all right.

The next obstacle to cross was the Gabes Gap, the ground between the coast and a big salt flat some miles inland. There were some Americans on the other side who were supposed to be pushing to the coast from Gabes, but it was taking them an awful long time and Monty started to organise the attack from the south. As usual the patrols went out and the remainder of the army took it easy. The guns moved up and units jockeyed round into position. The weather was good now and we were drilled* again, and had lots of lectures about malaria, as we were now in mosquito country. There was a lot of spare time and one day we bought two hens from a wog, at least we thought they were two hens, they turned out to be a cock and a hen and we kept them for months. Most of the tanks had a hen or two on, George had three, Stanley had two, but the tank commander, Jumbo, was a big eater, so one day they were hungry and did the hens in. Henry had some and Joe had about nine chickens. Middy had a big fat duck which he carried to Tunis, but gave it away. The fitters had about six hens and their lorry carried one right up until we sailed from Italy. They were great lads these fitters. At one time there was a sergeant in charge of them called Rogers and they got the name of 'Rogers' Rangers' and even when he went away the name stuck. There was Len the materialist, what a hard head he was; Dusty, hard working, he'd work all night on a tank if necessary to have it ready to start. Then there was Rocky Hazel, Dough, Johnny and Taff – there was always tea at the fitters' lorry, or something to read, or some good chaff. I see that I have forgotten the electrician, Walter, good boy Wally, what he doesn't know about automatic voltage control is not worth knowing.

We had a lecture from Fearless one day, the high command had been swopped round a bit. General Alexander had gone to North Africa as second-in-command to General Eisenhower and there were a few more changes. A letter was read to us from Monty which said that we would go on again together and the usual cocksure stuff he always says. It was good to hear it, there had been an idea in our heads that he was going, too. We were also told about the German Mark VI, the Tiger,[4] a sixty-ton tank with a stepped-up 88 on it. They were very bad medicine, but it was thought that if we ever fought them by having a superior number and doing some manoeuvring, we could make something of it. We did start to practise shooting at barrels – which might do some damage and part

---

* This means they went back in Khaki drill uniform, not that they did 'Square bashing'! *Ed.*

the commander's hair with a bit of luck. The high explosive shells for the 75 had a screw on the nose and when the slot is in line with a letter 'I' the shell explodes on impact, but if the screw is turned to a letter 'D', it delays for a second and a half. That enabled us to fire a delayed shot at a tank, it would hit the ground in front, bounce into the air and explode over the top of the tank. It was just a question of dropping the shell the correct distance in front, one and a half seconds delay.

On 2 April, after a terrific barrage and bombardment by aircraft, the 4th Indian Division and the Highland Division stormed the Gabes Gap in two places. We took very little part in it, just moved up ready to nip through, which we did on the next day, and started racing for Sfax. It was a good trip, but there was quite a lot of stuff to hold us up, guns and, in places, mines. The country was nice, groves of peaches and olives, not yet ripe, much to our sorrow. On the 8th we entered Sfax and were cheered and fêted by the civilians, it was quite a day. We camped about ten miles outside and visited the place twice. Stan, George and I had a haze on both times with drinking vin rouge, but we had been dry since Tripoli. We were all set for a long stay here, but one morning we moved out and did eighty miles north. Somebody had captured Sousse by this time, the Kiwis I think, and the Bosches were nicely boxed in up in that north-eastern corner with a line running from Bizerta round through Medjez-el-Bab to the coast at Enfidaville.

That day we drove through the Holy City of Kairouan. The Arabs make pilgrimage here yearly just like Mecca; seven visits qualify the visitor for a green rope on his headgear and he becomes quite a big shot. It was full of Yanks when we passed and we shouted down to them that their worries were over as we had arrived. We stayed here for a day or two then moved to the line and made a little attack, it got some ground but there were hills in front and we could not get far.

We moved from here eastwards towards the coast and put in another attack. It was successful, too, but just locally, there was only guns and a few tanks and they ran away. For about three days we sat on a ridge by day and drew back at night. On about the second day Big Ted was wounded by a shell splinter in the head, but not very badly. Lew, the gunner, put a shell dressing on it and we sent for the doc, who made him go back and stay the night in the ambulance. That made the third major and I began to think things over and decided that I'd better be a tank commander because there might be a fourth major, only it might be the driver this time: so I suggested taking the tank over. Ted said, 'OK', and a driver was sent for and I moved up to the top flat. The second-in-command took over, Captain Chave; he wasn't a bad guy but a bit nervous. He had been wounded at Derna in '41 and never quite got over it. Still, he took over C Squadron, but in a couple of days Big Ted was back and we all went back to our original places, me to changing gear. In this place we had a laugh one night, the RBs used to go out at last light away in front of the camp so that nobody could sneak up on us. They had tommy-guns and Verey pistols to fire up a red flare if there was any trouble and we'd all nip into the tanks.

This particular night a party of the Bosches came out to lay mines and they met the RBs – what a shindy there was, all in pitch darkness. The firing weakened us, once upon a time we'd have slept on, but I guess we had the habit of having one eye open, in any case the voice of a Spandau is a sound you can't mistake. It fires about a thousand a minute and is a fair machine gun even though the Bosches do make it. We all got into the tanks, but nothing came of it. Some more RBs went out and law and order was restored. After this we moved back, then east again right to Enfidaville and the hills. We sat here for a while, plans were being made to attack the place frontally and a sticky business it looked.

There were hills as high as Ben Lomond all side by side and the Bosches had guns on them all. We had Easter here and on Easter Monday the hen laid an egg, what a day that was, we were all dashing out like proud fathers. It laid an egg every day after that for weeks. On 28 April we had orders to paint the tanks dark green and cover up the desert rat sign with grease and on the 29th turned back and got on transporters. We travelled back to Kairouan, south then west and north to within thirty miles of Medjez. It took three days and it was a great trip, we sat on top of the tanks and whistled to the mademoiselles in the villages. When there was a puncture we

A young Jake with guitar and two friends, taken before he joined the Army.

A smiling Jake Wardrop, plus guitar, poses cheerfully with the rest of his recruits' squad at the RTR Depot, Bovington Camp.

An A13 cruiser tank of 5RTR at their Windmill Hill camp, where they had moved to from Perham Down, so that their barracks could be used to house a newly formed training regiment.

Cruiser tanks belonging to 5RTR ready to join in battle with the advancing German panzers, France, May 1940. (*Tank Museum*)

Men of the main body of 5RTR are pictured here resting on the dockside at Plymouth, shortly after their safe arrival from France.

This way to the Western Desert – or 'Up the Blue' as the 'Desert Rats' called it.

An inescapable natural desert hazard was the sandstorm, which came unexpectedly and blotted out everything. It could kill the unwary, caught without proper protection from its choking, swirling sand clouds.

'The Wire'. This battered fence marked the border between Egypt and Cyrenaica.

Lt Col Robbie Uniacke in the turret of his M3 light 'Honey' tank – note the enemy shells landing in the background of the photograph.

Good close-up shot of one of 5RTR's 'Honey' light tanks, the first lease-lend AFVs supplied by America to Great Britain. All 5RTR tanks had names beginning with 'E', it being the fifth letter of the alphabet.

German panzers arrive at Tripoli. Rommel made them drive round and round the town after unloading, so as to impress the locals with the size and power of the DAK.

Gen (later Field Marshal) Erwin Rommel, the 'Desert Fox', as he was called by both sides. Rommel was a charismatic and inspirational leader, who revelled in the freedom of manoeuvre which the desert allowed. Here he talks with German and Italian soldiers. Note that he is wearing British anti-gas goggles, which he found were excellent for keeping the sand out of his eyes. They became one of his 'trademarks' as he wore them constantly.

'Arco di Felini' (we called it 'Marble Arch') built by the Italians to mark the boundary between Tripolitania and Cyrenaica.

Lt Col Robbie Uniacke, CO 5RTR, talks with Brig Alec Gatehouse (late RTR), the commander of 4th Armoured Brigade, at a demonstration of the new Grant medium tank held in Egypt in 1942, for the then C-in-C, Gen Auchinleck.

Another photograph taken at the same demonstration, showing Maj Gen 'Jock' Campbell VC, DSO, MC, then GOC 7th Armd Div, driving the C-in-C (Auchinleck) in his open-topped car in which he led numerous 'charges' at Sidi Rezegh, where he was awarded the Victoria Cross. Brig Gatehouse is in the rear seat. (See Jake's remarks about him in Chapter 3.)

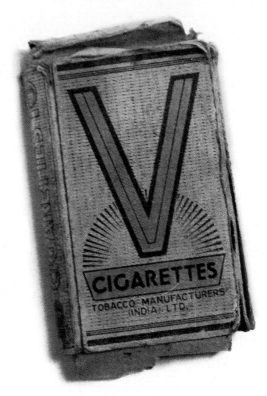

Victory 'V' cigarettes were smoked by all.

Grant medium tanks belonging to 5RTR, in the desert. The arrival of the Grant's powerful 75mm tank gun was a shock to the Germans.

The Squadron Commanders of 5RTR, just before El Alamein. Left to right: Bob Maunsell, Dick Ward, Alan Biddell and Paddy Doyle.

Gen Montgomery, wearing a slouch hat instead of his normal double-badged RTR black beret, talks to Lt Col Jim Hutton near Medinine not far from the Mareth Line. The photograph was taken soon after 5RTR had taken an important feature in front of the main German defence line.

Jake Wardrop (on left), with two of his best friends: George Stimpson (centre) and Stanley Skeels (with beret), in front of their Grant tank just before the battle of El Alamein, October 1942.

The End in Africa. The last of the Deutsches Afrika Korps wait to go into captivity, May 1943.

Jake poses proudly in front of his new Sherman at Homs. This was the M4, US medium tank which replaced the Grant. Its 75mm gun was in a fully rotating turret instead of a side sponson.

Ancient ruins at Leptis Magna, near Homs, where 5RTR were located to rest and prepare for the next battle, prior to going on to invade Italy.

A Sherman of 5RTR passing an Italian farmer on a dusty road in Italy.

Jake (minus shirt) poses with his crew in front of his Sherman 'Firefly'. Its 17pdr was extremely effective against all types of German panzers and was issued on a scale of one per tank troop.

Lt Col Rea Leakey, DSO, MC, who took over command of 5RTR in January 1945, when Lt Col Gus Holliman was killed, gives out orders over the radio. Maj Bob Maunsell stands just behind him.

Signboard for 5RTR's last wartime
location, taken just after VE Day.

POWs and wounded in Rethem. Maj Alan Crickmay, OC
'C' Sqn, is wearing the fur collared jacket.

Lt Col Rea Leakey and the officers of 5RTR are seen here on the steps of their mess, soon after
the end of the war in Europe.

Members of SHQ 'C' Sqn, 5RTR, pose with a Nazi flag outside Hamburg after the war had ended.

Jake's gravestone in the British Military Cemetery, Soltau, West Germany. The grave is flanked by those of two other members of 'C' Sqn, 5RTR, who were killed on the same day in April 1945. One of them, Tpr W.A. Forrest, was a member of Jake's crew.

made tea and begged rations from the dumps on the roadside. There was a joke made here by one of the lads, he had been given a tin of treacle duff, or something like that, and he came back with it in his hand saying, 'First Army, no wonder they can't fight, they're too well fed.'

We drove through a place called Le Kef one day and it was full of refugees from Tunis and Bizerta. They all turned out to see us and you should have seen the lads, they were peering at them with binoculars and whooping. Sometimes I used to think the sun had got us a bit, really it was just high spirits. We had come such a long way and we were going to Tunis now and we were good and we knew it! I'll bet the people of Le Kef will not forget the mad English who passed through that Sunday in the Chais-de-combat. We saw lots of Algerian irregulars here, hard looking cases they were, too, Foreign Legionnaires, Spahis, Indo-Chinese, the lot. On 1 May we got off the transporters and camped on the road. While we were here a few things happened: we saw Jock MacLeod and I became a tank commander.

When we arrived at this place, an officer from Jock's outfit came to see us, he had been in B Squadron before and saw the colours. The next day Red Haggis himself came, it was good to see him. They all rallied round to shake his hand, Stanley, George, Henry, Cliff, Woody, Middy, Len, Posty and George Carter. There was Snake Bite and Mad Coutts and chaps from the other squadrons all rallying round to see the great man. We pulled his leg, of course, about how fat he was on the First Army rations and wanted to know what he had been doing hanging around so long in the one place. Somebody pulled the old one about his worries being over now and to watch our smoke when we got going. Sad to say, there were a lot absent; it was a changed C Squadron from the one he knew.

We got a few more tanks here and I graduated to the top deck of a Grant. I was pleased because I'd changed gear long enough and besides I had been after this since Enfidaville. They were a good crew, George the driver, Joe – gunner, Frankie – loader, Woody – operator, and Jimmy, 37 gunner sure shot, Gillett. On 4 May we moved along the road to the place we were starting off from. That night there was a lecture for tank commanders at the CO's tank and we all went along. Fearless gave one of his usual speeches, I shall always remember the beginning, he said, 'Well, gentlemen, we are going to Tunis tomorrow', and then he enlarged on the plan. The 7th Armoured were operating with the 4th Indians; there were two thrusts, one of the 1st British Infantry and 6th Armoured Division, and the other ourselves and the Indians. One was First Army, the other Eighth Army, so there was a strong competitive spirit about the whole thing. There were plenty of guns and they were going to shoot up different high points for an hour: the infantry were to follow and as soon as they had reached a certain point we were to go through and not stop. He wished us all good luck, good hunting and we went back to the tanks.

It was a long way back to C Squadron and Henry and I stood waiting for a lift down the road. A jeep came in sight and I stepped out and started to thumb it. As it got nearer I could see some red and then some more, so I quit thumbing and saluted; there was a nice lieutenant general in the jeep and as he passed he saluted back and we piled in. The driver was a signalman from 9th Corps Headquarters and told me that the big shot was General Anderson. Bill Tudor was in 9th Corps and this chap knew him. I told him to tell Tudor he'd seen me and to watch out for me in Tunis in two days. This chap was quite amused, but I told him to listen to the six o'clock news the day after next – I hope he did.

At first light we moved off and got well up to the front, the Indians were doing well and, in fact, we were going through Bosche minefields at about nine. I saw Jock MacLeod once more, he was standing on the track as we passed and I gave him a hail. We had a quick brew, then the order came to move. The Indians had reached their last objective and it was all over. I like the Indians, when they do an attack it is an attack. They give everything such a good beating up that the Bosches are dead scared of them. If they happen to run out of ammo, that doesn't bother them in the slightest, out come the knives, they carry on and there are no prisoners – everybody gets done in. They certainly get into the spirit of the thing. I hope that they come to England for the next push, them and the Kiwis, that's all we need now. We passed them that morning sitting making tea and chapaties: they knew us, they knew the sign and they gave us a wave. They had taken guns of all sorts in their stride – there were 88s and 105s and stiffs all over the place.

That first day we made very good time and did more than half of the distance. We shot up guns and lorries and took thousands of prisoners. The RBs were rounding them up and just shoving them back to march on their own. Some of them thought they should be carried in lorries but the RBs put that out of their heads by beating them over the head with the barrel of a tommy gun and sending them on their way with a kick in the pants. There was some fair shooting, too, Cliff knocked two lorries off the road in two shots and Big Bill Beady is credited with a half track for six shots from the machine gun at five hundred yards, just one burst. Up in front the RAF were bombing anything that moved and we were bombed ourselves by the Yanks, at least we say it was them. For occasions like this we carry yellow smoke bombs and everybody was lobbing these on to the ground, but it was no use. We had one tank hit and three of the crew wounded, Goldy got it again, his third time, he never misses. He has bags of guts and was worried only that he'd miss the wine in Tunis the next day. At last light we camped by a farmhouse and Stan and I had a snoop round it. The people were still there and asked us to come in. We gave them some cigarettes and biscuits for the little ones and they gave us some wine, about two gallons in a can.

In the morning we cracked on again and by about midday we were sitting on a ridge overlooking the town and shooting up some guns. There were a lot of fires burning and we could see lorries baling out to the coast. The brigadier came up here in a dingo and he and Fearless had a chat about it. They must have decided to get going, because very soon after we moved down the other side on to the road and entered the outskirts of the town. There were Bosches and civilians on the streets and some resistance in houses, but a 75 through the window put a stop to that and we carried on.

We halted outside a place like a school, it was the Bey's Palace and everybody was just standing around, talking to the civvies and getting some order amongst the prisoners. We had a huge crowd of them by now, when someone opened fire from this place on the left. It was thought that we'd be better to beat it up a bit and two troops were sent off to work round the walls, find some more gates and go in, while Captain Chave and I went in the front gate. It was a bit like a park with fields and roads and here and there some buildings. We loosed off a few 75s at various windows and moved along the road, but the firing stopped and the prisoners came running out. A French civilian told us that there were prisoners of ours in one of the buildings, so we left that one alone. In every one of the buildings there were Bosches and we had to root some of them out with the tommy gun. The RBs had come up and were joining in the fun, we got Lugers, cameras, watches and rings. I got a pair of binoculars here. In one of the places there were the offices of the German consul and the RBs went in and gave the place a going over.

The big shot himself, a typical big squarehead, wanted someone to carry his kit and suggested that he should not be taken prisoner as he had some diplomatic status. He made an awful mistake telling the RBs that, they laughed at him and pulled his leg. They were saying, 'Carry your bag, mate', just like the kids at the station. When he was so mad that he almost burst his braces, they stopped kidding and slapped him gently with the tommy gun and took him away. Someone had released the prisoners by this time and they were a bit peeved, too. There were Americans and First Army chaps and they got hold of Bosche rifles and joined in. There were quite a number of the consul's staff bit the dust after that.

By about four everything was quiet and we stood around talking to the civilians. One of the high spots was an old lady with a revolver and a French flag who marched about fifty prisoners along and handed them over to one of the RB officers. She then presented him with the flag and kissed him on both cheeks, was his face red! The people were bringing out wine by now and they were inviting us to their houses to wash – the last one had been on the road near Medjez three days before. We gave them the cameras and watches we'd taken from the Bosches, as well as our rations, cigarettes and had quite a party.

That night we slept on the pavement by the tanks and Stan, George and I had a nice little session on red wine and brandy. The war was going fine, the Bosches had all been killed or captured and those who were loose had retired to the Cape Bon Peninsula, where the RAF were giving them a headache. Down at Enfidaville the Highlanders and New Zealanders had fixed up the crowd who were holding out there so the next morning we drove through the town and out to the east to see what we could do.

It was early, but the people were out waving to us, I guess maybe some of them hadn't been to bed very much the night before. It took us quite a while to go through the place and everyone halted, the people swarmed round giving us loaves of bread and bottles of wine. I think some of them got so excited that they will be nervous wrecks yet. We had halted on one occasion and I saw Simone, she was standing on the pavement waving a little flag and she looked great. I shouted down 'Good morning' to her, then nipped out of the turret to speak to her. Her mother and father were there and three sisters. I met them all and got her address to look her up when we returned.

We carried on through the town and we decided to have a breakdown, I slipped down to the driver and told him to pull in and let the others pass. The tank was going badly, it was old and the rings were worn and the plugs oiled up quite a lot. I called on the air for the fitters and we all got out of the tank to have a look round. The people flocked about us asking if we were the Eighth Army and where was the brave General Montgomery. We went to several houses and had something to eat. In one I had a bath. It was great fun. We had quite a lot to drink and the floor of the turret was covered with bottles of rum, brandy and wine: but the fitters had finished work and the war was still going on. So we wished them farewell and set off after the battalion.

They were busy clearing up the area between Tunis and the coast to the east and having a fine time. We captured airfields, hospitals and all the base depots of the Afrika Korps. The roads were full of prisoners, like an international crowd coming out. On the shore we rounded up some hopefuls who had expected to find a boat there waiting, including a crowd of Italian sailors. One of them had a guitar for a short time, as long as it took Stan to get to him and tear it out of his hands. He came whooping up the road to me waving it. That night we moved back towards the town and camped. We had a good party round the tank and invited some of the gunners and the RBs. We drank and sang songs until one in the morning and a good time was had by all.

That was the end of the trail; we did not fire another shot in anger in Africa. It had been a long journey and taken two years and five months and it was fitting that it should finish the way it did, with the desert rat division hammering through and ringing down the curtain on the North African campaign. We had fought in the blazing sun and in the pouring rain, in sandstorms and mud and blazed the trails across the blue, where even the Senussi would not venture. We had lived on salt water and bully and biscuits and had done long stretches in the tanks of anything from twenty to twenty-eight hours, and once it had seemed that we were beaten. But we were never licked. Sometimes we had fought and lost, but the spirit had always been there and when the time was ripe we showed them and we shall show them again.

The next day, we dug a hole for the bottles, aired our blankets and lay around making tea and sun-bathing. At one o'clock we moved back through Tunis and out to the west about six miles. During a stay here of three days we went into Tunis daily and I looked up Simone and her people. I took them to a wine shop and we had a mild celebration, mild I mean by certain standards, but, bless them, they probably had a great time. We all went home then and had something to eat and sat talking. I told them about my mother and sisters and Loch Lomond and all sorts of things. In fact, if I'd had another couple of bottles, I could have written a French-English dictionary there and then.

On the third day we moved south for sixty miles to a place called Bon Rada and camped again. Here we stayed for a week and once more lorries were run into town. Stan and I struck a good place here, or rather on one of our trips from here, a restaurant called the Max-Doll. We went in one morning and there were a couple of Yanks, they had arrived by this time, and these two were drunk and singing, so we just gave the manager the wink and bounced them. The place was full, but it was as smooth a bounce as I've seen and there was practically no commotion. When we got back in, the manager thanked us, gave us a bottle of champagne and told us to look him up any time; he was a good little guy. We went back there quite often and met some French people, all very nice and very sociable.

On another trip to town, Pete Broadbent, a very hard case in A Squadron, got hold of three great big barrels of muscat. We arrived at the car park and they were on one of the lorries. Pete did not say where they had come from, but they were there and that was the main thing. On the way home to camp, Stan and I were feeling dry, so we took the bung out of one and siphoned some more after that. We arrived at camp in high spirits and put the barrels by the tanks. The stuff lasted for a long time and when we moved, the water cans on all the tanks were full of it.

After three days at Bon Rada, we got on transporters again and the whole division took to the road. It was a good trip, right back through Le Kef, Kasserine, southwards to Gabes and Medenine, across into Tripolitania, to Zuara and Tripoli and finally east for seventy miles to Homs. Some wise men suggested that we had come to the wrong place and that the order that came should have been 'Send them home' but had been muddled a bit and was deciphered as 'Send them to Homs'. However, there we were and there we stopped for three months, the whole division, tanks, guns, infantry, engineers, all the lot.

CHAPTER SIX

Homs

Thanks for the Memory

Thanks for the memory, of the Berka and its bints,
The bootblack with the squints
The bloke who's just down from the Blue
His arm done up in splints,
How lovely it was.
Thanks for the memory, of camels and their humps,
Middle Eastern dumps,
Of Yankee beer that's far too dear, and gives us all the jumps,
How lovely it was.
Many's the time we've fretted
About cash we've betted,
But how in the Kiwi bar we've wetted,
We've drank wog beer with damn good cheer,
So thanks for the memory, of wog kids stabbing butts,
Eunuchs without nuts,
Of living in a country where we all got Gyppo guts,
Oh, thank you so much.*

Editor: After the capture of Tunis everyone in 5RTR, indeed in the
whole of 7th Armoured Division, was hoping that they would be

---

* From *Kiss me Goodnight Sergeant Major* by Martin Page and published
here by kind permission of Granada Publishing Ltd.

allowed to stay somewhere close to the city, so that they could, as the divisional history puts it: '. . . exploit such sources of amusement and relaxation as had been unearthed in the city' – and certainly Jake was no exception! But it was not to be and they were rapidly withdrawn into the desert to a wilderness called Bou Arada where there was no sign of life except for the odd cactus. Fortunately they did not have to stay there for long, the next move being Homs, on the Mediterranean coast, east of Tripoli. Jake did not think much of it as the diary tells; however, this is where the division was to remain while it got ready for the forthcoming operations, so like everyone else he soon made the best of it. There was of course the sea, sand and sun which made up for a great deal, there were also organised leave parties to Tripoli and Tunis, there were 'self help' amusements such as a race meeting with the local sheiks, and there was a particularly virulent type of date brandy for which Homs was famous. And in addition, of course, there was quite a lot of work to do. Some new vehicles had to be drawn up and the rest carefully checked and repaired. Jake replaced his high mileage tank for a new Sherman. All the associated equipment, like radio sets, charging engines, etc, had to be given a good going over. Then it was necessary to get down to individual training, to brush up on those essential skills such as personal weapon training, which tend to be all too easily neglected. There was also training for seaborne landings, training in waterproofing vehicles and training in the tactics of fighting in close country – quite a change from the desert.

The main operation for which the whole 7th Armoured Division was busy training was the invasion of Italy. They were not used in Sicily, although the divisional commander, General Bobbie Erskine, and a small tactical headquarters did take part, with the intention of providing a controlling headquarters for the independent armoured brigades operating there, should it prove necessary to weld them together. As it turned out this did not happen, and after about two weeks in Sicily, the GOC and party returned to Tripoli. As far as the complete division was concerned, they were initially scheduled to take part in Operation Baytown, Eighth Army's landing on the toe of Italy, but later were switched to Operation Avalanche, Fifth Army's landing in the Gulf of Salerno. Fifth Army, or to give its full title, 'The United States Fifth Army', had been activated in French Morocco on 5 January 1943, and was commanded by Lieutenant General Mark Wayne Clark, who had already shown great personal gallantry, when he was secretly landed by submarine on the coast of North Africa, to coordinate details of the forthcoming Torch landings with the French. It is difficult to imagine a more cosmopolitan army than Mark Clark's: it contained American, British, Commonwealth and French troops, and later on both Italians and Brazilians. Even the US army units contained the renowned Nisei battalions composed of men who were of Japanese–American descent.

While in Homs the 5th were visited by His Majesty the King on 20 June 1943, and lined the route to cheer him when he arrived. They also said a sad farewell to their extremely popular Commanding Officer 'Fearless Jim' Hutton on 15 July, firing their tank guns in salute when he left. His place was taken by Lieutenant Colonel R.N. Wilson. Final preparations were made in early September and it was decided that the 131st Lorried Infantry Brigade Group, comprising two infantry battalions, 5th Tanks, a battery of 3rd Royal Horse Artillery and a troop of Royal Engineers should be the first troops of the division ashore. Fifth moved with the rest of the division from Homs to Tripoli where they boarded the landing ships which were to take them to Salerno.

Sergeant Jake Wardrop

I suppose we could have been put in a worse place than Homs; those I can think of off-hand – the North Pole, Devil's Island or the middle of the Amazon jungles. It was a place with a population of perhaps two hundred, one main street with some lemonade shops and a few quite nice villas down by the sea. We were camped about five miles to the east on the shore. On the north side of the road there was a cultivated patch of palm trees, water melons, limes and beans of different sorts, with some huts scattered about. There was a track leading through this patch and from the edge of it to the sea was about three hundred yards – that is the place we lay all summer. Between the camp and the village lay the ruins of Leptis Magan.

The Italians had excavated a lot of the place and built quite a nice building just off the road in which were all the small stuff like pottery, coins and so on. Here I suppose in peace-time some Italian had quite a nice job taking liras from the tourists and showing them around. It was a wonderful place, the building nearest the sea was a villa with great high pillars and tiled floors. Behind this was the arena with the seats in a semi-circle and rising up like a football stand. There were baths and temples, I could never find anybody who knew much about the place, so I don't know myself. There were some more excavations at Zabrathe, about sixty miles to the west of Tripoli and at Carthage, just outside Tunis. There is a lot of Roman stuff lying around that coast, back to the east at Cyrene near Derna and Marble Arch. I heard a tale about how that was built once.

Away back in the old days there was a dispute about where the frontier should be between Tripolitania and Cyrenaica. The two best marathon runners at that time were two brothers, so one was taken to Tripoli and the other to Benghazi. At a given day and time, the two of them set off to meet. It had been arranged that a line running south from the meeting place would be the frontier. Well they met at the place where Marble Arch now stands. It must have been an exciting finish, with both of them trying to get an extra few yards for the other side, because the spectators got so worked up that they bumped both of them off and having buried them the Arch was built and that's the reason it is stuck out in the blue miles from nowhere.

There is a lot of history attached to the Siwa Oasis, too; it is two hundred miles south from the coast and is a lovely place with springs and hot baths. I have never been there, but Big Ted had been when he was in the Long Range Desert Group[1] and he told me about it. There is an oracle there and a lot of the old-timers used to take a trip down to see if there was any luck about for them in the next two or three years. Alexander the Great went there, also Mahomet went when he fought his Western Desert campaign in the sixth century. Cleopatra and Mark Antony had a weekend there too. It must have been quite a place.

Another interesting place is the Kufra Oasis, which is in the Sahara six hundred miles south of Benghazi. Up until the war the only two Europeans to get to it were a German explorer early in the century, 1906 I think, and Rosita Forbes about 1930. The Long Range Desert Group did it often and there was a joke about for a while that they used to go there on leave instead of Cairo.

Most of the wogs living in the blue west of Mersa Matruh to about Marble Arch are Senussis; that is they belong to a religious sect formed by a man of that name round about 1880. They are all Mohammedans, but this old boy thought that they were not taking it seriously enough and formed this band. He forbade them to drink or smoke, insisted that they read the Koran and that they should pray five times a day and be good boys generally. Well, it went over big, they joined in and carried out his orders. When the Italians came to the place, they had a very difficult job with these lads who fought them and never gave up. The Italians used planes against them, armoured cars and lots of troops. They cemented the wells and in 1936 when Graziani was Governor of Benghazi, thirty a day were being shot. But the others fought on and hid in the rough hilly country to the east of Benghazi and shot up Mussolini's legions as they passed along the roads. When the Italians entered the war there was a Senussi Force founded and they continued with the scrap, and good lads they are too. The old man who started it all is still living, I think, and during the scrapping he stayed in Alexandria. I think the Italians put a price on his head. Maybe he will be back now on the blue again, sitting by a fire and looking at the stars. He must be a good old boy.

But it is about the end of May and we are sitting at Homs. We still had our tanks, but moved into Troop areas with tents, or if somebody had no tent he built a little shelter out of groundsheets and that kept the dew off at nights. I was in Headquarters Troop and we had four crews, less the officers, who all slept in an area together. Behind us was 11 Troop, Henry and Cliff; behind them was 9 with Snowy and Digger, and on the left were 10 with Joe and Ted and 12 with Jumbo and Bertie. In the middle was the cook-house and near it the Quartermaster's lorry. We ate together here as a squadron, sitting on the sand like wogs in the sun. Up on the edge of the cultivation, the fitters had built a hut of boards, galvanized iron and sheets. It was a great little shack, just like a beach-combers hut on one of the islands.

We did nothing for weeks but sit in the sun, swim, read and eat. At night we'd sit around listening to the wireless or go to Leptis to see a concert. There was some beer, most times two bottles per man, but there were always some who didn't want it and Stan, George and I did miles running round to see who didn't. The sergeants had a bottle of whisky occasionally and I bought Ted's as he didn't drink it and it came in handy. The first excuse for a party was the return of Dixie from South Africa. He had gone away some time before. By good luck he arrived on beer day and we had a nice little session that night. One day somebody had a brain-wave, to build a Mess Room, so that we could sit down to eat. We got a few lorries and scoured the countryside for weeks and it was surprising how much there was. There was enough to build a cookhouse, dining-room and a little Officers' Mess, so now we had our meals from a table sitting on a form, all our own work. One day we built a raft, it wasn't a huge success, but we had a lot of fun making it.

One day we had a lecture from Lieutenant General Horrocks, the last phase in Tunis. It was for all the officers of the division, tank commanders, armoured car commanders, gunners, infantrymen and engineers, it was very good. He had been in charge of the Indians and 7th Armoured and was pleased at the way it had gone. He thanked us all at the end and praised us up and finished it by saying that the handling of the division had been superb and if he ever had another job to do, he'd have the same combination again. He was wounded later on by a plane strafing, but is doing well I hear.

In the middle of June we started to run eight-day trips to Tunis, this was inclusive of time for the journey, so whenever a party went, they hammered the whole way only stopping for petrol, punctures and food. As soon as one driver got tired, another would take over, they'd go all night and there was a record for the trip which everybody tried to break. The distance was about seven hundred and the record, never broken, was twenty-five hours. Which wasn't bad for a three-ton Ford with fifteen in the back and maybe a blow-out thrown in.

At the beginning of July Major Doyle came back to the unit and took over C Squadron again. He looked none the worse for the donk on the head and had been in India and Syria. There were a few changes in the unit here. The big one being Fearless left us. We all paraded so that he could say goodbye and thank us for the DSO he had received for his brilliant leadership since Alamein. He made a speech and went. We lined the track and cheered as he drove out and three Shermans down on the shore fired a salute. As he passed I could see that he was crying, Fearless Jim who would have taken on all the Bosches in Germany on his own. The Major of A Squadron also left us here, Major Ward. He also got the DSO and was a great guy. He is now a lieutenant colonel and has a bar to the DSO; he got it in Italy. Big Ted took over his squadron and Biddy was still commanding 'B'.

I went to Tunis on leave and had a great time. Jimmy went with me and we stayed at Simone's house. They were all pleased to see us again and we took them around a bit. One day we hired a car and took the family to the seaside. We had a picnic and went swimming, it was great fun. The old man marked time on us so that we did not do much drinking, but an odd time we sneaked off and had a session. There is a lovely swimming pool here and we went a lot. The trip back was good, we just failed to break the record – it took us twenty-five and a half hours. It had been a good leave, I enjoyed it very much and I think the family did, too. We all swore eternal friendship and I have to see them in Paris, *après la guerre*.

Back at Homs things were the same. It was July and the weather was super and everybody was so brown that it was impossible to get one shade darker. I used to look round Leptis at the concerts just when the sun had set, at all the lads sitting there. It was a sea of brown faces and arms, bleached hair against a background of khaki that was faded almost white with the sun, didn't they look good. There was a memorable night when we drunk a lot of gin at the fitters' shack. The canteen had come and we spent the afternoon whooping around raising all the stuff we could and by night there was a formidable array of bottles. The snag with the gin was that we had no lime or lemon and it was rather like drinking Brylcreem, but we stuck to it and after a bit nobody cared. All the habituals were there, Stan, George, Dixie, Henry, Cliff, Pooky, Alf, Tweeny and some more. It was a full moon and down on the shore the surf was pounding on the beach. I had a guitar and we sang 'Aloha' many times. It even seemed to me that the drink was right, it couldn't have been whisky or beer, gin was the stuff. We all lay very low next morning and about four went swimming – what a night.

After this, Stan and I went on the wagon and started training to fight for the brigade. We walked on the road in the morning and evening when it was cool, did PT on the beach and knocked one another about with the gloves. The contest was a scrappy affair, it was too hot to box really, and some of the lads were on leave and the elimination took time: but the field thinned down and Stan and I were still in. We scrapped about six times. In the contest we drew to fight the Div RASC and lost by one point. Stan had a knock-out in the second round, but I went the distance and scraped it on points. The finals were won by the Queen's Brigade, they were held in Tripoli and there were some good scraps. Shortly after, we held a swimming gala, an inter-battalion one, in the brigade. There were five teams, 1st Tanks, 5th Tanks, 4th CLY, Royals and 5th RHA and we won it. We had some good swimmers. I made up the number in the relay and got a second for lifting the plates. We also played some water polo and had some good fun in spite of the fact that there was no pool. Instead we used the space between two LSTs which were pulled up on the beach about fifteen yards apart.

About the beginning of August we started to equip again: the campaign in Sicily was drawing to an end and we all had a pretty good idea where we would be going next. The Highland Division had taken part, also 30th Division and the 4th Armoured Brigade. The tanks with big mileages were taken away and we got new ones, tracks were renewed and things started to move. I got a Sherman and the crew were Stan driving, Carlo – machine gunner, Jimmy – 75-pounder, and the old Pathan Woody – operator. We did some shooting and 'Sure-Shot' Jimmy blew the targets to pieces at any range. All the old hands were there again. The ones who had sworn that they were finished after Tunis, the bugle blew and they were off to war. Henry and Cliff, Snowy, Digger, Dixie, Ted, Joe, 'slap-happy' Joe, who went to Headquarters Squadron, and we had some pretty good officers. The Major, Captain Burt, Captain Boon and the commanders of 9, 10, 11 and 12, Messrs. Heywood, Eckersley, Osborne and Daniels. My old commander from Mareth was back and he was second-in-command of the battalion.

Two chaps came from REME one day and gave a demonstration of how a Sherman could be waterproofed to drive in six feet of water. They fitted a cowling over the air intake, extended the exhausts to stick up in the air, plugged everything up with putty and pitch, and sealed down the driver's and machine gunner's flaps. It was then possible to drive in right up to the turret which they did one Sunday morning. We all turned out to cheer or laugh, depending on whether it was a success or not and just in case, a tow rope was shackled to the tank on the beach. It was a huge success; the tank reversed right in until the water almost went into the turret, then came out forward. They did it once more for good luck and the experiment was over. Within a week all the tanks in the battalion had been treated for taking to the water except for some finishing touches which were to be done in the Tripoli area. We started to buy rations for the campaign, sausages, tins of steak and kidney, and all sorts of stuff like that. Below the turret the tool box was crammed full of tins, we hoped that at least we would get a chance to eat some. About this time we lost a very good sergeant major from the squadron, Jock Ramage, he went up to RSM. We got Busty from A Squadron – but more of him later. Another change was the Quartermaster. Nippy came to us from Headquarters. The staff remained the same, Fairy and Jock. George had a change too, he came from 12 Commander to the Major's tank and is the big-shot operator of the squadron.

On 27 August the tanks were packed, the work was finished and we were ready to go. It was great, the lads were frisking around like dogs with two tails, our spirits had soared sky-high again. That day the canteen came again and by the old ruse Stan, George and I got five each of beer, which was better than nothing. We had a little party for a farewell to Homs, that delightful seaside resort.

CHAPTER SEVEN

Italy

Editor: The US Fifth Army, when it landed at Salerno, comprised the British X Corps and the US VI Corps, the former being on the left of the assault. Lieutenant General R.L. McCreery, who had been Chief of Staff to Alexander, was commanding the corps in place of General Horrocks who had been badly wounded in an air-raid on Bizerta. X Corps comprised 46th and 56th (London) Divisions who were to be used in the assault and 7th Armoured as the follow-up division. 5th Tanks began landing at 1915 hours on 15 September on Sugar Beach, Salerno, and for the first few days the beachhead was jampacked solid with men, vehicles and equipment. The leading elements of the assault divisions had had some tough fighting, and the whole area was still under fire. For a while the situation was an anxious one; however, once the Queen's Brigade landed the division had an adequate reserve. At the same time, the Eighth Army had been pushing up from their landing beaches in the far south of Italy, to achieve a link-up. This was managed on the 16th, the Eighth Army having covered 300 miles in seventeen days against considerable opposition and many demolitions.

The bulk of the division was now concentrated some four to five miles from the coast around Battipaglia on land reclaimed from the marshes – hence the mosquito problem which Jake mentions. Although the precautions were tiresome they were very effective and malaria never became a problem in Italy. Concentration was completed by 27 September and the advance through the mountains north of the bridgehead began, with 23rd Armoured Brigade (consisting then of only one armoured regiment (Royal Scots Greys), an armoured car regiment (KDG) some artillery and sappers) attached to the division. Infantry support was provided by the Americans as and when required. The advance started on the night of 27/28 September, 5RTR and the 6th Queen's taking Scafati and holding the vital bridge over the Sarno River there against all comers. The route then divided around Vesuvius, 23rd Brigade taking the coastal road direct to Naples, while the main part of the division went around to the north, making for Capua on the River Volturno.

The leading armoured cars of A Squadron KDG entered Naples on 1 October, while on the northern route 22nd Armoured Brigade took over the lead once the country began to open up. 1st Tanks, 5th Tanks and the 4th CLY took it in turns to lead, and on some occasions even managed to advance with two regiments on parallel routes. It was hard going, as the German positions were always well sited and difficult to pin-point as there was plenty of natural cover – vines, tall maize in the fields, trees, etc. The weather was bad – leaden skies, containing rain which turned the fields to mud. Booby traps and road-blocks abounded and the bulldozers were constantly in use filling in craters.

The Volturno was reached during the first week of October and an assault crossing made on 12 and 13 October in the area of Grazzanise by 7th Queen's; their history records that they were greatly assisted by the fact that nearly every man had learnt to swim while at Homs! A bridge was started on the night of 14th/15th and a raft (to carry Jeeps and anti-tank guns) completed and soon operating. Meanwhile, 4CLY had found a fordable site just upstream which could be used by waterproofed Shermans. They managed to get two troops across on the evening of the 16th despite torrential rain.

By the 22nd both the British X Corps and the American VI Corps were established across the Volturno and had begun to advance towards the next main enemy delaying position which was the River Garigliano. This line was to be the limit of the division's advance in

Italy. In early November the division was withdrawn into reserve behind the Monte Massico feature, leaving 1st Rifle Brigade with just one squadron of 5th Tanks, and a squadron of the 11th Hussars, to hold the front some 4,000 yards short of the river. They were finally all relieved on 7 November and rejoined 22nd Brigade at Aversa. By now, news that the division was going home had been received and they happily handed over their vehicles to the 5th Canadian Armoured Division. There followed a brief rest period in the Sorrento Peninsula, with leave trips to such places as Capri, Pompeii, Vesuvius and Naples.

The main body of the division was embarked at Naples on 20 December on three ships, the 5th going on the *Cameronia*. The voyage home, as Jake explains, was uneventful, despite German propaganda claims, over the Rome radio, that they would 'prevent the return home of the 7th Armoured Division'. It was on 7 January 1944 that the division docked at Glasgow and were then moved by train to their new 'home' in the wilds of Norfolk.

So ended another chapter of 5th Tanks' war. They had faced many dangers in two very different theatres of war – the deserts of North Africa, the closer country of southern Italy. They had yet to face the most civilised and yet at the same time probably the most difficult terrain of all, namely the *bocage* country of Normandy. In the meantime, after three and a half years of almost continual action abroad, they could savour, for a few brief months, the undeniable pleasures still to be found in their native land.

Sergeant Jake Wardrop

On 29 August we got on transporters and set out for Tripoli as we were going to sail from there. We left about two in the afternoon and made slow progress. Still we were on the road again and it didn't matter how slow the race. The bridges, blown early in the year by the Bosches, had not all been built and at the deviations we had to take the tanks off and drive them round, then get on again. At ten we halted and made tea and a stew and lay talking and smoking. It was a lovely night, the moon was up and we did not get to bed until well after twelve – it was a fine evening. The next day we got to the four kilo stone from Tripoli and pulled off the road on a spare piece of ground beside the Lancia Works. Stan and I baled into town, but it was the same: a few more lemonade shops and one or two more bars. That night there was a fire in the harbour and a couple of barge loads of ammunition went up. They were tied up just in front of the Miramare Theatre and shells were bursting on the roof. I hope they shook some of the bugs out of the seats. We stayed here for two days and they were the funniest two I've spent. The tanks were bunched up close and only about two yards off the road. All the crews slept and cooked meals by the tanks and we always had an audience of British troopers, American Italians, or worse, all of them together. There we were, the mad dogs, stripped to the waist with no hats on making tea or pancakes or stew. Some would be reading or lying in bed and always there would be two or three kicking a football around and knocking the tea over. Then the language, Oh dear! There might even be a fight and all the time the sun smoked down and the wogs would look at one another and nod as if they were agreeing that we were mad. I met Pasquale one day: he passed on his bicycle and I gave him a hail. He runs a laundry now for all the troops who live around and does well. I asked if he had any brandy, but he said times were hard but he'd see what he could do next day.

The Divisional Commander got all the officers together one day and gave them an outline of the next show and later we were all told, 'the Division is going into the American Fifth Army along with two British infantry divisions and the whole thing under command of General Mark Clark, the American'. He was a bit of a dark horse as nobody knew much about him except that he landed in North Africa and did some snooping around before the Yanks and First Army got there. Still, we thought it would be a change and maybe we'd get some of these pansy American rations.

We moved from here to a place off the road where the finishing touches were put to the waterproofing. It was a grim area, dirty and full of flies and we were all jammed up tight together in a great heap. At nights we lit fires and sat around singing. The wogs seemed to enjoy it, some of them would come across and sit around. They were tickled to death one night at Coutts. He speaks Arabic very well and sang the song 'Igri Igri Igri', an Arabic love song: they joined in and clapped their hands. It was Ramadan[1] now and for a month they fast until the sun sets then sing and eat and have a party every night. A few of us went down to Pasquale's one night and had a session on the brandy, it was good and we had to walk home. Another day I called on the Senora to see how she was doing. She looked tired and worried, poor woman, and she shrugged her shoulders and said that Italy was finished. She had a better idea than most of us: although the papers had said nothing, all that fiddling around for an armistice had been going on for a while. On 3 September, the BBC announced that British troops had crossed the Straits of Messina and were scrapping in Italy.

One night a bunch of Swahilis came to the camp and did some war dances, they were good, too, shields and spears and great long drums – all the trimmings. They do it every night just for fun, but they will go anywhere to put on a show. By day they build roads and bridges and they sing when they are doing that too.

On 8 September we heard that the Italians had jacked in and all the tripe about Mussolini and Badoglio and all the short changing and double crossing that had taken place. The next news of note was of an Allied landing south of Salerno, that settled it. From that time on we knew exactly where we were going. On the evening of the 10th we had a last canteen, we were moving in the morning. It was a good party, the atmosphere was just right and there was enough to drink. I have been to a lot of these parties before operations, when everybody is keyed up, nobody seems to get drunk: it is just as though it is not having any effect except to make them talk. Probably the talk is to boost themselves up, you see, there is never going to be as bad a show as some other one, or so we say: then somebody recalls another incident and it is agreed that it was some show. That's the way the talk goes, until about twelve o'clock and everybody is saying what a piece of cake it is going to be in the morning.

On the 11th we moved to the docks, the ships were in and we started loading: as fast as one ship was full it would pull out and another would pull in. Even so, it was the next day before C Squadron was on and we pulled out into the harbour to wait until the next day, which was the 13th but by good luck not a Friday. I stood at the rail and watched the African coast receding. Goodbye Africa, we were away at last. A lot of things were running through my head just then, no more sand, there would be trees and houses all over the country we were going to, not just a little bit on the coast. There would be another language to learn and perhaps the mandolin. I even found myself speculating on the time it would take to reach Calais, where there would surely be a boat to take us home: but it seemed such a long way that I gave up and thought of pleasanter things – the Clachan or Dow's probably.

These LSTs[2] are fine ships; the accommodation is good and it was a grand trip after the sand of Tripoli. The lads in the Navy don't do so badly either, they can enjoy life generally. Of course, they take a lot of chances but things are quite pleasant in between. On the 14th, looking to the east we could see the Italian south coast and on the west Mount Etna. It did not look very spectacular, as there was a lot of mist and it was just visible. In the afternoon we went through the Straits of Messina, quite narrow and watched the barges crossing with supplies from Sicily. There was very little to see on the shore, the houses were maimed with bomb and shell splinters and a good number had been destroyed. The people appeared to be straightening the place up a bit now that it was all over and now and again one of the lads would spot a signorina with the glasses and there would be 'Where?' Then it would be, 'Do you see that house with the red roof, right a hundred yards, there is a rowing boat lying on the beach? She is just walking past it.'

That night we were told that the division would operate with the 46th and 56th and that on the beach it was backs to the wall, Stukas by the score and a lot of other tripe.

I was interested in the 46th, Arthur was in it somewhere I had heard from a lady we both knew, but I did not see him. On the 15th we reached the beaches of Salerno and Stanley was killed. It was a bad finish after ducking them for so long and he would not have wanted it that way, I'm sure, rather he would have gone out in the tank laughing and shouting as he had done so often. It will take a lot of squareheads to settle up for Stan!

By night the whole battalion was fit to travel, the waterproofing stuff had been removed and we were packed and raring to go and we moved about a mile or so inland. The Queen's were landed also and the ships returned for the 1st Tanks and CLY. The mosquitoes were bad: if anyone tells you that they bite only at night and sleep by day, don't believe it. The Italian brand are up all day long, they have a real party at sunset and for about two hours after and then settle down. I spent quite a number of nights in the turret and found that about one o'clock there were no mosquitoes and none throughout the night until just before light, when they came out again. We had been warned about malaria and had been taking meppachrine for a time before leaving Africa; we also had nets. A few of the lads caught it, but I noticed that the old drinking gang were immune. This may just have been a coincidence, but at any rate it was a good excuse for drinking the vino. Most of the lads I spoke to who had been here some days before us said it had been very rough, but I could never be sure. Salerno was eight miles to the north west, up the coast, and the nearest place was Battipaglia, this had been lost and won several times and we've finally bombed her into complete ruin with the RAF. It was in a mess, too, there were holes in the roads that could have held three Shermans and the whole place was flattened. The outer edge of the bridgehead was being held by the 46th and 56th and on the night of the 17th the Queen's and 5th Tanks took over and they came back.

On the 18th the Queen's were reported to have had patrols as far as five miles ahead, right up on the mountains. They had captured and killed quite a number of Bosches in the night and beaten up some guns which had been shelling the bridgehead for days. We were getting a bit of the new continental fighting already. The night of the 17th the battalion split up and a troop of three operated with a platoon or company of infantry. We had never tried this before, but it was the way we carried on all the time in Italy, except for the times when we took the lead and scorched along the roads. On the 18th we pushed further inland and got to Battipaglia; it had been held last by the Bosches, but there were quite a number lying around who would not hold anything any more. We had our first experience of the Italians at a little place just beyond. They had been here all the time, these people, and there had been a lot of scrapping in the area. Two men had been wounded and the doc came in the ambulance and took them away. That created a good impression and later in the day they brought us tomatoes, walnuts and onions. They were very reserved and, I'm sure, very frightened. We gave them some cigarettes and bully and they seemed quite pleased. That night at half past eleven we moved a few miles and sat around an aerodrome which was now being used by the RAF. It was a nice place by a stream and we were told that it was likely we'd be there for a few days.

Inland from Salerno there were two roads into the mountains, one along the coast to Naples and the other went round Vesuvius to the east and north. Both of these were held by the Bosches and infantry attacks were being put in on them, then we would go through and see how far we could get. We foraged around and got potatoes and tomatoes and two chickens and had some mighty 'scoffs' in this place. Before leaving Africa, we had been given enough rations for five days, plus what we had bought and were well stocked. Gilly came up with the office and we wrote some letters and listened to the wireless at nights. It rained on the third day, a real torrential downpour. The stream rose and during the night a lot of the tanks had to be moved and most of us were washed out. The next day was fine and the sun dried our kit until two in the afternoon when we moved.

The two infantry attacks had gone slowly but had reached the objective and it was time for us to carry on. We drove through Salerno, which is quite a nice place, and up the road to Vesuvius. This was the job we had come to do, the breakthrough and the dash, stopping for only long enough to fuel and make tea. It was a safe bet that the bridgehead was ours now or we should not have moved. It had not been too bad, at least when we got there it had been going for some days and I don't really know, but chaps I spoke to who had been there said they had seen worse. The Luftwaffe had been very quiet, a few times a day three Mes would slip in from the sea with a bomb each, drop it and run. Everybody laced them, Bofors, tanks, rifles and Bren guns and up above the Spits and Lightnings were hanging around. Not many got back. That night we pulled off the road and slept on the pavement. A Squadron were leading, then B and C, and that night tanks of A were fired on.

In the morning we got away at first light and C Squadron jogged along in the rear while A and B made the pace. They had some fun too, and by night B had got across the bridge at Scafati before it could be blown and A had exploited further to the north. It was at Scafati that afternoon that the three newspapermen were killed by fire from a Bosche tank. Things had gone well for the first day and we camped at night beside a jam factory which had been burned out by the Bosches. We opened the door and had a scout round and found sacks of sugar, tins of tomatoes and peaches, so we took what we wanted and left the rest to the civilians. It rained that night and we all got wet through again.

In the morning C Squadron took the lead and we shoved on to Scafati and up the road. George Harvey was killed that afternoon; poor George, the tank was hit by a self-propelled gun at short range. We got it and carried on to a place called Poggiomarine which was being held by the Bosches, they had quite a lot of guns, some tanks and a few 'Moaning Minnies'. I had not heard one since Mareth. We got all around the place by night and the Queen's went in with the bayonet and the tommy gun. We watched a bunch of them going up the road on a night fighting patrol. There were ten of them dressed in shirt and slacks, no equipment, rubber-soles, black faces and armed with tommy guns and grenades – did they look tough! As they passed the tank one big rangy lad looked up and said, 'I'll bring you an 88 back in the morning'. Next morning we pushed on, round the village, we were still leading and we got quite a distance before night. The Queen's had been through the village during the night and sorted out everything in it. They are very smooth workers. Among the booty were two 'Moaning Minnies'; it was quite a catch. The Bosches were getting jumpy and running away now and we made good time. They were laying mines, too, but the Italians in many cases had watched them and warned us, it was good of them.

On 1 October we hit a place called San Gennaro, we skipped round it so fast that we caught some Bosche lorries baling out to the north. Jimmy did some very sweet shooting, two in two shots and only one went on fire. From the other we collected some stuff, pairs of shoes, two sacks of sugar and a sack of potatoes. The people had been very badly treated; the Bosches had machine-gunned all the cows and horses and shot one young lad about fourteen years old. Some of the prisoners we had collected were the reported hard cases of the Hermann Goering Division. We handed them over to the RBs who led them away and looked after them!

On 2 October the 1st Tanks took the lead; they passed us early in the morning and we tagged along behind. It was a change and great fun.

One village we passed through, I forget the name, we halted on the edge of the pavement. It seemed a long halt so we nipped out and started to make some tea. I was sitting pumping the stove and I looked up and there were a couple of smashing Italian girls coming down the road with an elderly lady, their mother I thought. They passed the tank and I nodded and they carried on, but must have plucked up courage to speak by the time they reached the front where the lads were standing. The next thing, Woody gave me a yell and when I got round to the front there they were trying to get a lift to Napoli, which had been taken by this time. They were staying in this place because of the bombing, but had a house there and wanted to get back. Their English was not so good but we managed with some French and what a pair of smashers they were. We gave them some tea and said how sorry we were but were not going that way and I was sorry, too. We said goodbye and carried on.

The next day we dawdled along, still behind the fight, stopping now and again, making tea and talking to the Italians. I was sticking in to the language and doing quite well, it is so much better when you understand what they say and can answer them back. That afternoon we arrived at a village and halted again, the 1st had cleared it and were pushing on into some trouble at a place called Cardito.

That evening I went for a stroll round and passing a house the lady invited me to go in. There were three of us, Red, Carlo and I, and we had a wash and some vino, then met the family. There was a daughter called Rosetta, and she was very nice, we got on very well, also a few aunts and uncles. It was a nice house, too, but they did not have much to eat, so one of the lads went back to the tanks and picked up some bully, sugar and a sack of flour. That settled it. Out came the wine and some nice liqueur, stuff called mandarino. Each drink I took improved my Italian until about eleven o'clock when we were all firm friends and had discussed Mussolini, Badoglio, the King and Queen and a few other people. We slept by the tank and in the morning went to say goodbye as we were leaving at eleven. I got Rosetta's address and promised to stick in at Italian and write to her. Goodbye Rosetta, *bella signorina*.

The CLY had taken the lead and we followed on behind. The previous day the 1st Tanks had captured Cardito[3] after a terrific scrap in which they lost eight Shermans of one squadron and six in another. They had pushed through the vineyards and bumped some well camouflaged SP guns. They knocked a couple out and we had a look at them – 105 millimetre guns firing solid shot mounted on a tank chassis. They were very low and hard to spot in the trees, they are pretty bad medicine. We pulled off the road that afternoon and stayed for a couple of days. The CLY were scrapping around Aversa and a lot of stuff was moving up the road to take part in the battle which was anticipated for the River Volturno which lay ahead. There were big American guns, 7.2 inch and 155 millimetres, towing along at a great pace. Our old friends from Africa, the 4.5s and 5.5s were going up, also loads of the 46th and 56th lads. When we moved the battalion took the lead again and made for Capua, it was being strongly held and about seven miles from it a bridge going over a fairly wide canal had been blown. The engineers fixed it and we carried on for another mile and turned down a quiet road to the left.

Ahead lay Capua and the river and on the other side there were mountains. I thought the Bosches were slipping a bit for not shelling us as we came up the road, then turned up towards the river again. We were now on the fields, cross country stuff and it was raining. The going was heavy even for tanks and a number of them got stuck. Each troop of tanks took over a frontage of about four hundred yards and we were told that there was nobody in front but the Bosches. Squadron Headquarters was a bit behind in an old castle and each troop was on the air all night reporting hourly to the major.

We spent the night in the turret, guns loaded, all keyed up for an attack which never came. It's a funny sensation standing looking into the darkness for the Bosches, every tree appears to move and I found myself about to open fire time and again. In the morning I laughed at myself for being so jumpy, but the next time it was just the same. It rained all day and the area around the tank deteriorated in about six inches of mud, what a mess the tank was in. There was a good bit of shelling and some 'Moaning Minnies' but not very near us. Here I had my first experience of Rita, Mr Heywood, our troop officer.

He had joined us at Homs, just an ordinary lieutenant from Blighty and as was always the case with new ones, he was a bit of a joke. He turned out to be a good officer and a great guy and I remained with him until we came home. That afternoon he went for a stroll round and found some Jerry ammo dumps and poking around he found that each one had a time clock to blow them up. He walked round them all, removed the clocks then called on the air for some engineers to be sent up. The clocks, of course, were never meant to be found; they blew up in the explosion and were the first the engineers had seen and a very cunning device they were. The rough shape was like a potato masher with a rather big head made of bakelite. The top part held the clock which had a face marked with figures of days and minutes. The shaft of the thing held the striker and fuse and at the end it had been threaded so that it could be screwed into a slab of gun cotton. Thus when the Bosches were baling out, one of these clocks was taken, wound up and the dials set to perhaps the fifteenth minute of the third day. It was then screwed into a slab of gun cotton and placed in the middle of the ammo dump, where it ticked away quietly for three days and fifteen minutes and then, bang! It went off and if you happened to be around you didn't drink any more vino. It was quite a good show of Rita's and I was pleased for him.

The next day we were ordered to go forward to the Volturno and see what we could see. Off we went, very steady, nearer and nearer, until we were within four hundred yards of the river. Out hopped Rita and taking the tommy gun he set off into the trees, just like Daniel Boone. I wondered how he would get on and kept on my toes to back him up with some 75, but in about ten minutes he was back. He reported on the air that he had been to the river and seen nothing, so we hung on until night and went back to the place where Headquarters were camped. It was a good place, this old castle, with a big courtyard and walls round and we pulled into the place as the rain came on. It was not very clean inside, but at least it was dry so we baled in and it turned out to be a good job we did. During the night the Bosches shelled it and one or two chaps who slept in the yard were wounded. It was funny to be shelled in the night and so accurately. I guess they must have registered on it before. We all got up, walked around and had a chat about it, where the shells were coming from and so on and then went to bed. The walls were thick and I pulled my bed in close to one and went to sleep. The next morning I went to see Dixie. He had been hit in the eye with something, a piece of earth or stone, the day before when some shells from a 'Moaning Minnie' dropped near. He was fine and did not go to hospital. It was a good job that it had been earth and not a splinter or he would have lost an eye.

Later that day we pulled back to an old stable or riding school about a mile north of Aversa. The Volturno was going to be a full-scale show and guns and infantry were being brought up. By this time the bridge had been blown and the Bosches were sitting on the north bank. On the road down there was some shelling and some transport was knocked out. The road was bad, too wet and slippery and there was some stuff in the ditch. The weather was fine and we started to get cleaned up a bit when we halted. The tank was full of mud, our bedding was wet through and we had a lot of work to do. For a week we remained in the stable and it was quite good. The rations came up every two days and we worked a bit, ate and wrote some letters. Aversa was a good place and we soon found the wine shops. They sold vermouth, muscatel and an egg and brandy mixture called Baton. We gave them a lot of business and I pounced upon the Italian and got to know some civvies. There was not much to eat for them. Naples was being used as a port and flour was being brought in but it had not reached Aversa at that time. I was sorry for the little children and gave away a lot of our rations, in fact we had some rows about it. The argument always ended with me giving a long speech about being thankful that these conditions did not exist at home. I would have given the lot away. Very seldom since Italy have I been really hungry, I guess I lost my appetite.

From here I fled into Napoli and had a look round, it was good and I am glad I saw it. I went to the cathedral of San Gennaro, saw the Castle Nuovo and climbed the hill to the north and looked down on it all. It was dirty and some damage had been done by bombing, but it is a good place considering that it had been wide open for four years. Having a constant stream of troops milling through for a few years does not improve it and besides there had been a fight for it thrown in. The Bosches had blown up the lights, gas and water supplies and that did not help. It is nicely situated, too, in the middle of Naples Bay, away to the south the coast runs down to Sorrento and Amalfi. They are nice places, beauty spots and I went to see them later. Just a few miles out from Sorrento is the Isle of Capri, I'd like to have gone and seen San Michele but I'll have to wait until I look up Pasquale when the war is over. Vesuvius dominates the whole scene, it stands just behind Napoli and can be seen from anywhere around the Bay. Four thousand feet it is, always smoking sometimes thick black smoke and others as though it had stopped. Down on the front is Santa Lucia where old Axel Munthe went to swim and cool his head after battling all day against cholera. I liked the people too, they sing and play the mandolin and have a good time. I became a sergeant here, not that it mattered but I qualified for a bottle of Vat 69 now and again and that was something. At this place too, we had a shuffle round of the squadron and I went into 9 Troop; Rita was Commander, there was Snowy Harris, the glamour boy of the *Picture Post*[4] and myself. Snowy is a stout lad, they don't come better and we got on very well. It was a good troop, the best we always said, of course so did the lads of 10, 11 and 12. It was a good thing too, that friendly rivalry, and kept everybody on their toes to do something better than the next. I have not mentioned before, but Henry was acting troop commander at this time, we were a bit pushed for officers just then and since we came to Italy, Henry had commanded 11 Troop, three tanks. This was not an uncommon thing and a few old hand sergeants have done it, but never for as long as Henry.

On 17 October we moved north to Santa Maria, a place about ten miles from Capua and a little to the east of it. The attack had gone in a few nights before and two bridges had been built across the river. The one at Santa Maria was an American pontoon one, but the Capua one was a British built Bailey Bridge and carried a notice to the effect that it was built by so-and-so Royal Engineers and was the first Bailey to be built operationally. There had been others, but that was the way across to the Germans, we could not have reached them without it. Round about this time we began to wish Monty was around; the Mark Clark stock dropped right down. Here we were at Santa Maria, the bridge had been built and all that happened was 9 Troop crossed over and on reaching the other side were recalled. On the 18th we moved into the town and camped in an old Italian barracks; it was quite good. The town was small but we nipped around it and got some brandy. Rita was pushing round and came back with several crates of beer, birra Peron's, an Italian lager; it was quite good. We had a little session round the tank and got quite lit up.

One night I was out and I got tangled up with some Italians, I don't know how it started. It was just a little house and I went in and had some vino, then sat around talking to them. As usual the vino was speeding my brain up and we got on well. I had picked up a big dog somewhere and it was trailing around and it was in the house too. They were interested in the dog and said that there were not many in Santa Maria as they had all been eaten. Probably they had an idea they'd like to eat this one, but I pointed out that the dog was my friend. He was a very brave Scotch dog, I had had him for ten years and he'd been in Tripoli and all over the place. This put them off, but I went and fetched some bully from the tank and that helped. After a while I baled out with the dog and it went home and I went back to the tank to sit in the turret and read. I read a very good Howard Spring book here, *Fame is the Spur*.

On 21 October we moved at 4.30 to Capua across the bridge, the town had been bombed to pieces, but the civvies were back clearing up the houses. It was an operation this time and the 5th Tanks were leading, we had to capture two villages, Sparanise and Francolise. As we moved up the road, the stuff thinned out until we reached the artillery positions. Past them for about a mile then we pulled off the road. Ahead of us was the infantry line, the 56th, and about four we had orders to move out and back some up for the night. So a troop set off, Rita had all the information and Snowy and I trailed along behind. The road was being shelled and if you ever want a queer sensation, try standing in a tank with your head out of the top going along a road which is being shelled about quarter of a mile ahead. We were going slowly and making no dust and I didn't think we could be seen, so it was better to just trickle along. In any case, it's always a toss-up, an extra long one might get you, so we carried on nearer and nearer. My heart was doing about a hundred and fifty per minute and just to pass the time I spoke down to the driver, sweet nothings like, 'You're doing fine', 'Keep her going steady' and such like tripe. We made it, one landed just ahead and about ten yards later another just behind. I asked the driver later if my voice sounded queer and he said he didn't hear a thing, the mike had gone dead – they do that sometimes.

A few hundred yards further on we pulled off the road where there were some Hampshires with some machine guns and a couple of six pounders. The British front line, a troop of tanks and a few infantrymen, I thought of Monty again. He would have had the Highland Division screaming across the fields with the bagpipes and a couple of tank battalions battering up the road. That finished me and General Clark; he might be good at snooping around the back streets of Oran, but he couldn't run a good company of Girl Guides. We sat chatting to the Hampshires, they looked a bit lonely there on their own and were pleased to see us. Late that night they pulled out for a rest and we held the fort, sitting on guard in the turret, guns loaded, tensed up, eyes straining, but nothing happened. On those nights in the turret, listening and waiting and watching the Plough swing right round the Pole Star I thought a lot. The plan for the capture of this dump was to send a troop of tanks down each road and leave them to it.

At about an hour before the dark we were ready to move, by that I mean we had cleaned our teeth and started up. We hit the road, did about a mile and swung across country to another road which led to the town. It was breaking light just as we reached the road and who should be there but a bunch of Bosche infantry. I gave Jimmy the tap to cut loose with the Browning, just to stop any jiggery-pokery and the ones who survived it stuck their hands up. Snowy and I nipped down and rounded them up with the tommy guns. They were a punk-looking crowd, white and thin and they said they were Poles. I don't know if this was a sign for us to make some tea for them, but we rang up on the air for somebody to come and get them so that we could carry on. We worked up the road to the town and found it impossible to go any further than a railway bridge across the road which had been blown down.

I stayed there while Rita and Snowy worked round across country. Snowy had a few belts of Browning and found some more infantry and settled the hash of quite a number. There was a hill at the back of the town and we were shelled from it, but not to any extent. A couple of carriers of the Recce troop were with us and the two commanders went on foot into the place. They came back soon saying that they'd been fired on by a Spandau. Snowy and Rita were making no progress, so they came back and we parked in some trees out of the way.

About eleven we decided to have a look at the place, so Snowy and I pushed in on foot. We went along quite a way and met some civvies who said the Bosches had gone, so we carried on. We were walking up the street and there lying at a doorway was a Spandau, so we made a run for it. Just then a Bosche stuck his head out of the door, saw us and we opened up. He ducked back but kept putting his hand out to pull the gun in and he got it. I only had my revolver and the damned thing only holds six rounds. I ran across the street to try and get a shot in the doorway. Just as it gave a last click, Snowy had fired his last round from the tommy gun. I've thought since we might have rushed the place, but the crying need then was for a Mills bomb, I'll carry two in future. Snowy looked at me and I looked at him and we both tore down the road. Every minute expected to hear the Spandau open up, we had two hundred yards straight to run. But no, I guess we scared them, if nothing else.

About an hour later a civvy came up in a great state, he had come from the village and was talking about a lot of Germans there. When I asked how many, he made fifty with his fingers, so we crept up to the bridge to have a look. There were quite a number, walking along the pavement and going into houses. So I watched which ones and ran back to the tank. We pulled forward to a position from which the gunner could see the houses and then he went to town on them. It was nice shooting, Jimmy dropped an HE into each top storey window, then each bottom one. I watched with my glasses, but nobody came out. I'll bet they don't go hiding in other people's houses again. About three o'clock Rita decided to stage an infantry attack, so two men were left on each tank and the other nine, armed with tommy guns and revolvers, went in again. I was with Snowy and we snooped around the gardens and saw nothing. We were beginning to think they'd gone. We were going along a road, on the right was a bank about three feet high and a field on top, Snowy gave me, 'Sh! Here's a Bosche walking towards us in the field', but he hadn't seen us. We decided to catch him and sneaked along a bit further to snaffle him. The road we were on joined another one about ten yards further on and just as we reached it we spotted another Jerry coming down it. Without any more ado, Snowy gave him the works and the cat was out of the bag. I dashed up the bank and cut loose at the other one in the field. By this time he was heading for the tall timber and I'm not sure if I got him or not and we didn't wait to see. He dropped, then Snowy and I did a strategic withdrawal. This time there was some Spandau, but we were well down and got back across the railway to the tanks. Just beside the bridge there was a railway station and we had a snoop round it. It had been burned out, but in one of the buildings there was a safe. I visualised it as being packed full of thousands of lire notes, but we couldn't lift it.

Nothing much happened that afternoon and as it got dark we pulled back quietly to camp with the squadron. The place we stayed at was about a mile down the road and right along a smaller road, it had been blown up and we diverted across a field. The whole squadron went round one behind the other and the last tank ran on a mine which blew the track off, you can never tell. The show had gone well enough, the troops had gone along the different roads and in each case had been held up by mines or demolitions, but they had pushed on and had some fun and passed the day.

The next morning we were up and away before light and crossed the fields again. This time we decided to try another place, we pushed further round the village and approached it warily. The reconnaissance on foot by commanders was indicated and we pulled in beside a house and pushed out with the tommy guns. There was Snowy, Jumbo of the carriers, an old C Squadron man, and myself – this time we took some grenades. There were deep sunken roads all over the place, trees and fields. We were stalking quietly along one of these roads and there in front on the bank was a pair of feet sticking out of a nick cut in the bank. All together we bore down on them and pulled out a very startled Jerry, who had been writing a letter. We chased him around and set off back with him to the tanks. A call on the air soon produced a dingo and our captive was taken away. He was a Panzer Grenadier, one of the supposed tough babies. I'll bet he keeps his eyes skinned the next time he is on guard.

We moved forward a bit then with the tanks and ran into some quite heavy and accurate shelling. It was obvious that we needed some infantry, but they did not arrive, so Rita and I tried again. You see, one of these SP guns could have knocked the three of us off in as many shots and Rita refused to buy the dummy. This time we got very close to a Spandau and did nothing much except get a scare. We had to run, Rita and I, that made my third time since the day before. We bummed around for the rest of the day, and an OP from the guns came up. We had some fun working our ranges with him while he passed the messages back on the air to the guns. That night we camped in the same place and watched a Beaufighter get a bomber with one burst, it was nice shooting. He must have been hanging around waiting for them to come back from a raid on Naples, they always flew north.

Next morning we were up again and before we started, Rita got Snowy and I on one side and said that he was going in for the kill as we had messed around long enough. It was a bit of an anti-climax. We drove round the village, through the trees and on to the high ground beyond the place. We were there. Rita wirelessed back that 9 Troop had reached the high ground beyond and what had to be done now. At the same time over on the left B Squadron had reached Franolise and everything was fine. The brigadier came up in his dingo and told Rita he was pleased about it and he looked it too. I saw the report on the show which Rita made as troop officer. It said that,

It is quite possible for tanks unassisted by infantry to operate in close country. If necessary, the commanders must dismount and push forward on foot. This was done time and again by Sgts Harris and Wardrop, who showed considerable initiative throughout the operation.

Snowy and I got ourselves a bigger size in berets next day! That night the RBs took over the ground, dug themselves in and guns were brought up. To the north there was a plain stretching for about ten miles to Isano and some more mountains. It was thought that the Bosches had retired to these and already the 11th Hussars were feeling out to see what was there. There was a sequel to it all. Two nights later the BBC announced fresh gains by the Americans who had captured the town of Sparanise after three savage counter-attacks. Snowy winked across at me and we smiled. We camped the night by a farm and pushed around next day in a dingo to have a look at the place. At the scene of our duel in the street there were no bodies, but chips – knocked out of the door? I wonder. I took a look in the house we shelled, too. Dear, dear what a mess! The safe in the station had been bothering me so we went there to see if we could open it.

After this I shall stick to bully beef tins. We battered it and kicked it and finally put a hand grenade under it, but in the end we gave it up and went away disgusted. I guess we could have used about five minutes of Simon Templar's time that day.

I think perhaps that round about this time the big shots were thinking of taking us home, because about a couple of days later we moved right back across the river at Capua again and west to a place called Villa Leterna. At about five we arrived and put the tanks in a field. The crews slept in a disused hotel, it was raining. That night Nippy came up with the rations and Arthur had two bottles of brandy, so we had a little session in the back of the wagon, Nippy, Arthur, Jock and I. It was raining outside, but the inside of the wagon was dry and it looked fine after the first bottle had gone. There was nothing much doing and we did our washing and wrote some letters and sat around. One day I baled out and jumped a lorry to Napoli. It was on this trip that I met the lady whose father worked in Farraris. She was nice and so was the cognac she was selling. There was a great amount of American stuff coming off the ships, self-propelled guns, half-track Whites with a three inch mortar and some M10 tank busters.[5]

One day we were all confined to camp and that night we moved, or rather it was about two the next morning, and what a trip. It was pitch dark and raining, but as the daylight broke, we were waiting at the bridge at Capua, making tea inside the tanks with the stoves. We had come thirty miles in the dark. Nobody had hit the ditch and the whole outfit was present and correct. To the north-west there were some hills and we moved up to them through a place called Concello, which had been bombed flat. There were concrete pill-boxes, four feet thick, split right in two by direct hits, it had been nice bomb aiming. Up at the sharp end the Queen's were in the line with the RBs and 1st Tanks. It was nice around here, farms and houses with cows and sheep in the fields. The Bosches must have gone in a hurry to have left them. In a farm nearby they were digging up the valuables they had buried in the fields. All the bed clothes, clocks and stuff like that. The fitters' White was parked in the farmyard and I used to go over to listen to their wireless and talk to the Italians. For about three days we sat there and then moved up a bit nearer to a place called Mondragone. The 1st Tanks had a lot of tanks in the mud and we took over. It was a bad place really. A road ran along the coast, while on the other side of the road was quite a high ridge running round the coast. It didn't give us much room to operate, rather like fighting up the Lochside beyond Tarbet. There were streams running into the sea and in every case the bridge was blown. Mines had been laid and there was a gun or two to hold us up. We moved forward steadily, each night the engineers filled up the road again and lifted the mines until we got round to the Garigliano River. To the north was Cassino and Rome and it was here that the advance fizzled out. It looked like being a repetition of the Volturno, as indeed it turned out to be.

On 10 November we had a parade and the CO told us we were going home and read a letter from the divisional commander. It said that the 7th Armoured Division was coming out of the line, going into imperial strategic reserve and, if the situation in Italy got no worse, we were going home. What a day that was, you should have seen the smiling faces. Two or three days later the advance party of the Canadians arrived and we started to go back, a unit at a time. The 46th and 56th stayed behind, but I have no doubt that they will come soon. The 14th saw us moving again right back over the bridge again and south almost to Aversa. We pulled into a place called Faitiles and camped in the school. It was a good little spot. There was a wine shop which sold a brew like cider made from passion fruit and a fighting drink it was. I got to know some people, they had baled out from Napoli because of the bombing and I used to go there at nights. We had started to eat at the cookhouse by this time, as we were all together. I gave these people a lot of rations we had on the tank, biscuits, bully, cheese, sugar and stuff like that. We kicked around here for a while, cleaning the tanks up and wishing this boat would hurry up to take us home for Christmas. Amongst other things that came to light when we cleaned out the tank was a bottle of rum and one day Woody and I started to drink it about nine in the morning. It was raining and cold and we just had a nip to keep out the flu. Well, after that we had another and maybe some more. Busty, the sergeant major, joined in, he had a bottle of Marsala and we passed a pleasant few hours digging, talking to Lieutenant Garnett, who used to be a sergeant in C Squadron.

Carlo got into trouble here; he smacked an MP, not just an ordinary one but an RSM. Well, he went inside and stayed there for a while. Jimmy, the gunner, was tangled up in it, too, so that left Woody, Harold and myself in the crew. Still, the war was over for a bit for us. The thing dragged on for some weeks and ended in Carlo having a court martial, defended by a very slick officer from A Squadron. He got off scot free and the MP got a rap over the knuckles for being so frivolous, poor man.

On 25 November some of our tanks were handed over to the 40th Tanks. They had come across from the Eighth Army front on the east coast and had been having some good scraps. The CO used to be in the 5th, he played rugby in the forwards and was a very tough baby. We had seen this crowd before, it was them who crossed the wadi at Mareth and had gone into Tripoli with the Gordons. They are quite a good outfit. A day or two later some of the crew moved off down the coast to Sorrento and Castellamare and shortly after we drove the rest of the tanks to a dump in Napoli. It was a good trip. We waved to the signorinas and laughed when the lads on the pavements shouted that we were going the wrong way. Wrong way, indeed! On 2 December the rest of the unit moved to Castellamare and we sat there for two weeks.

C Squadron was camped in a red jam factory which had been blown up by the Bosches, and a very good job they had made of it. I don't suppose the place will operate for months to come. It was a good spot and I met some people, quite a number. The first was a Canadian who could play the guitar and sing just like Roy Rogers. I met him in a wine shop and saw him by chance one day on the road. One day I bought a guitar in a little shop, the one from Tunis had become a bit worse for wear. The owner of the shop was a lad called Antonio and he was a wizard on the guitar and mandolin. He invited me to come to his house any night and we could have a little jam session. His father and two brothers also played the strings and he had three sisters. One was married and living in Rome and they used to worry about her a lot. They also had some smashing gramophone records and we used to hear them often. I got a lot of instruction from Tony in the guitar and in Italian, too. They called me Giovanni and I went to dinner with them a few times. The cooks in the squadron were continually weeping about the bread and rations that were missing every morning. I used to cane them, what did it matter, we didn't starve and these people were hungry. I have their address and when I learn some more Italian and it is possible, I shall write to them.

Nearby the 1st Tanks were staying in a big house and we visited them, then sent invitations to them to visit us. Many good nights were enjoyed by all and a lot of vino was consumed. There were some hospitals in the area and the personality kids, I mean the officers of C Squadron soon got chasing the nurses. One night I was coming back from the 1st, hazed a bit, guitar at the slope, jacket over one arm and had reached the door when Jock came dashing out and led me away to one side. He said there were some sisters in the Mess, to watch the language and so on. He was in quite a state. I got organised a bit and went in and there they were. Five English Sisters, looking clean and slick, sitting at the table. We sent out for ten bottles of vino and had a sing-song, it was very good. At that time there were seventeen of us sleeping in one room, Busty the Sergeant Major, Nippy the Quartermaster, Len, Dusty, Joe, Ted, Cliff, Sam, Jerry, Digger, Pickles, Stan, Ernie, Jack, Snowy, Dixie and myself.

It was a good steady life, but some of them were becoming mighty hard to live with. Many times there were invitations thrown out to step outside and a few right hooks were swung. I knew what was eating them, it was the waiting and it was wearing them ragged. All the time we stayed there I did not fight in the Mess. If I felt like that, there was usually a Yank hanging around and he did instead. I used to patronise a wine shop near the camp which was used by some of the RHA men. There were some hard cases in this crowd. They had been abroad about six years and were quite mad. Many a night they would sing the English county songs, 'Lincolnshire Poacher', 'Ilkley Moor', 'Bladon Races' and songs like that – the English equivalent of 'Loch Lomond', 'Dark Lochnagar' and so on. One chap sang 'Here's Good Luck to the Barley Mow' very well, it's a grand song. I liked these gunners, they were sun bleached blond-haired killers and great guys, not many Scotsmen either.

Each morning a crowd of civvies came to the factory, the manager, the assistant manager, a few workroom men and a very nice signorina called Pia. We got to know her quite well. She had a sister called Ina and they came to dinner a few times. Both of them were very nice, but poor lassies, they were hungry. I pinched many a loaf to give them and plenty of bully and stuff like that. One night we had a good party, I asked Tony the Guitarist to come to the camp and bring some friends. He turned up with guitar, mandolin, violin, accordion and drums. We had some vino laid on and sent invitations to every camp in the neighbourhood. Some of the ladies from the hospital turned up, officers from the Queen's and 1st Tanks and some of the lads produced a few signorinas. It was a good night. We danced, drank and sang songs until the band went home, leaving the mess full of people. Most of our officers were there with the sisters, all of the sergeants and Jock Reid who is the Brigade dentist. He is a great guy and comes from Coatbridge. Everybody knows him for a good dentist and a fine chap. He is known as The Fighting Dentist. We had a session that night and recalled memories of Lauder's, the State Bar and Green's, he knew them well.

On 17 December we got on the train and moved to a place called Casoria, from here it was five miles to Napoli or thereabouts. We lived in tents, very rough too, but nobody minded much as the boat was near and a few of us still had hopes of being home for New Year. We were forbidden to go to Napoli and, in fact, were almost confined to camp for the four days we spent here, but I baled out each afternoon to go and see Rosetta. The day we hit the place I checked up on the map and found her town was only ten miles away, so I was off like a shot. They were glad that I had remembered them and pleased my Italian had progressed so well. I could speak to them and get the hang of what they were saying. We swore eternal friendship and I broke all the rules of security by telling them I was going home soon. I got the address and promised to *presto ritorne* when the war was over. Goodbye, Rosetta.

On the 20th we got up at 3.30 and marched to the docks at Napoli. The big job was finished and another one would be starting soon. We had done well enough in Italy and had the valuable experience of operating in continental conditions. That was the reason we did not come home after Tunis, we had to be introduced to the conditions on the continent, so different from the desert. And we had done so. We had learned some new tricks and improved on the old ones and now we were going home. There had been a lot of speculation about where we would dock, but I knew. I knew that morning when we got to the quay and I saw the ship, the *Cameronia*, and why not. I had set off from Prince's dock and I'd go back there. It turned out that I was wrong by about a penny one by tram, we landed at Shieldhall. It was a good trip; on the afternoon of 20 December we pulled out of Naples harbour.

I was standing on the rail looking at Vesuvius and thinking of a lot of things. It had been good fun, the Italian episode, and I'd enjoyed it. Would I ever go back? Away to the south-east I could see Capri where San Michele stands and I had not seen it. I thought of them all, Rosetta, Antonio, Gemma, Pia, Pasquale and Lincino and thought of the Italian song 'Come back to Sorrento'. Maybe . . . maybe.

On the way out of the harbour a ship came in with troops lining the rails. I got the glasses on it and who should they be but the tough lads from the North of Africa, Algerian irregulars. I had not seen them since Tunis. They had the same old cloaks of brown and white stuff and the big black beards. It did not take them long to hit the news either, about ten days later the BBC were announcing pushes by French troops in the Cassino area. On the ship we had 1st Tanks, 4th CLY, 11th Hussars, 1st RBs, our medical unit and 5th Tanks. It was jokingly remarked that the troops on the *Cameronia* were the best that ever took to the water together and if the Bosches had known they would have nipped a few Focke Wulfs over to fix our duff. It was a dry ship but Dixie and I have overcome this by pinching a jar of rum at Casoria before we left. I carried it on board in my bed roll and never was a bed roll handled more carefully.

There was a lot of boat drill and turn-outs for imaginary U-Boats' attacks and it irked a bit. The OC Troops was a lieutenant-colonel and he had his eye on an OBE I think for safely taking troops around. He used to sit in his office and guff over the wireless for hours about nothing. By good luck the loud speakers had a plug and whenever his voice came over 'Attention, please, OC calling', out came the plug. The amusing thing about it was that everybody came under his orders, the brigadier even and all the COs of units. It was quite a big convoy and the escort was American destroyers.

On 24 December we pulled into Oran harbour, the whole convoy came in and the escort ships. It appeared that we had to wait for some ships to come from Alexandria. The destroyers tied up alongside and the GIs came on board to trade cigarettes for souvenirs or buy lugers and berettas. They were good lads, they are just the same as ourselves when you meet the right ones. The boys driving around in jeeps about fifty miles behind the line are just windbags, but these guys were scrappers and the same as ourselves. They had three subs to their credit, several planes and an armoured train which they beat up at Salerno. I got to know one whose name was Clasen, a great big Swede. He was a torpedo man and said, 'Call me tubes' (pronounced toobs). He and two pals came aboard and we gave them a lot of junk out of our kit bags. They were all for buying the stuff, but we wouldn't take their money. On Christmas Day they went ashore and at night came back on the ship with two bottles of cognac, which along with the rum made a little party. Toobs knew a lot of songs, but had a voice like Wallace Beery. However, he sang 'Pistol Packin' Mama' and 'Stagedoor Canteen' and we gave him a big hand.

There was an incident that night which made me think a lot about these Yanks. On the *Cameronia* there was a little naval rating, a signalman, and somehow he got down in our place. That would have been all right, but he started to talk too much and tell us where he had been and what a tough baby he was. Even that wouldn't have mattered, but he started to run down the Yanks and especially Yank sailors and that was very bad taste. Well, big Toobs just put his hands in his pockets and stood there laughing at him; it was a fine show. To end the incident I bundled the noisy one out of the door and hung one on his chin and that finished it. On Boxing Day we went for a walk to Oran, but I go too fast.

Later on Christmas Day, very much later, the Americans had gone and we were all in bed, there was a terrific commotion in the cabin. I wakened up and there was Rita, good old Rita, drunk as a lord and with two bottles of champagne. He and Mr Hammond had been ashore and had a day in Oran, a very good day by the look of things. Dixie, Digger and I gave them a hand with the hooch while Rita scouted down to the galley. He came back with pieces of turkey and chicken and we all had a nice Christmas supper.

The walk to Oran was good, it rained all the time, but I enjoyed it. It is quite a nice place and I wish we could have stayed longer. While we waited a convoy came in from England, Black Watch and a few English country regiments and lot of Artillery, a division I should think. We gave them a good welcome, you should have heard the cracks. Maybe they were heading for Italy, but could an army not be gathering for a push to the South of France, *quien sabe?*

On 27 December we pulled out from Oran and dashed through the Straits of Gibraltar. We did not see a thing as it was dark, the next morning the African coast was still in sight astern. We were bearing due west into the Atlantic to avoid the Condors. This time it was goodbye to Africa. I watched it sink lower and lower on the horizon until at last it was gone. No more sand or Senussis, farewell to Cairo and Alexandria, the Golden Bar, the Sweet Melody, Ceophis and the Washington, it had been good fun.

The following days were dull, there was no land to be seen and very little to do. In the Azores vicinity a couple of fighters flew around for a while and later we saw the odd Hudson. I spent the time reading and tearing into the guitar tutor, trying to get the hang of E, G, B, D, F, slow going. Each morning Rolly and I did ten laps of the boat deck before breakfast and another ten before dinner. New Year was dry, but there had been dry ones before and what did it matter. At twelve o'clock I was wide awake lying in bed reading the life story of Mustafa Kemel, the Terrible Turk; he was quite a lad.

On 4 January there was land on the starboard all day – the Irish coast. We pushed around it steadily and about five o'clock I could see the Giant's Causeway through the glasses; ahead lay the Mull of Kintyre and the Firth. There were still a number of optimists who thought the ship was going to Liverpool, Avonmouth, and a few more places, but I refused to take their money. The 5 January broke fine and before it was light we were all on deck. The ship was at anchor and as the dawn crept up from the east, there it was on the starboard beam, the Clock Lighthouse.

I was home.

Editor: The diary ends here. I do not know if Jake continued to keep one in North West Europe; if so, I have so far been unable to trace it. Certainly he still kept what he had written with him on his tank, but no new entries have come to light.

The Last Battle

It was April 1945. Seventh Armoured Division, as part of XII Corps, Second Army, was engaged in the last desperate battles against the crumbling Third Reich. They had crossed the Rhine on 27 March, their ultimate objective being to capture Hamburg, some 200 miles away. Pockets of enemy resistance were continually being met en route and the savage fighting which took place was every bit as fierce as it had been earlier on in the campaign.

One such bitter engagement took place near Rethem, located on the River Aller, south-east of Bremen. Here 53rd Welsh Division had met heavy opposition on the outskirts of the town from men of the 2nd German Marine Division, whose positions covered crossing sites over the river. They were supported by 88 mm and 125 mm railway mounted flak guns, which made them an even tougher nut to crack. Two attacks on their positions had been repulsed, 5RTR, who had been concentrated with the rest of 7th Armoured east of Nienburg on the River Weser to the SW of Rethem, was sent forward to assist. It was during one of the subsequent battles near Rethem that Jake Wardrop was killed.

After returning to the UK from Italy, the 5th had spent three months drawing up new tanks and training hard with them for the coming invasion of Normandy. They were re-equipped mainly with Cromwells which many considered to be inferior to the Shermans they had left behind in Italy. However, there were in each squadron a number of Sherman Firefly, which was an adaptation of the American Sherman M4A4, which had been rearmed in Britain with a 17 pounder gun. Initially they were issued on a basis of one per troop, and it was true to say that the Firefly was one of the very few tanks landing in France that could take on a German Tiger or Panther on anything like equal terms. Jake, now a sergeant tank commander, had the Firefly in 11 Troop, C Squadron.

In a letter written after the war, General Bobbie Erskine, who had been commanding the division in Italy and had taken them over to France, wrote about the fundamental differences of outlook between troops like his veteran Desert Rats, who had been fighting continuously since the beginning of the war, and those who had never been in action before and were desperately anxious to win their spurs. As he put it: '. . . It was no use trying to pull the wool over their eyes, they knew war too well to take it lightheartedly.' One can imagine how difficult it must have been for men like Jake, who had been almost constantly under fire for four years, to have to get themselves ready for battle once again, knowing that they had probably already used up at least eight of their nine lives. But they did so, without complaint, and it is a credit to the men of that great division that they were able to come to terms with the new conditions, so different to those they had left in the desert and Italy, and to go on to win fresh laurels.

By the time he got to Rethem Jake had yet again been at the 'sharp end' for a very long time. There had been no 'cushy desk job' for him, to relieve the tension-filled days of tank commanding in action, not knowing what lay around the next bend or over the next crest. He must have been very tired both mentally and physically, but perhaps his spirits were buoyed up with the knowledge that they were definitely on the last lap now. The war must end soon, if only he could stay alive to see it.

One of his best friends was Sergeant George Stimpson, who had known him since pre-war days at Perham Down. 'Stimo' told me that the night before Jake was killed they had had a drink together and a chat. This was a regular occurrence; even though they were no longer in the same tank crew, they still tried to meet at the end of the day, probably when the squadron had gone into its night leaguer, to exchange a few words and smoke a cigarette. 'I managed to do this the night before he was killed', said Stimpson, 'and we talked of the many friends who were no longer with us. In retrospect I feel that Jake had a premonition of what the next day would bring, but we still managed to knock back a bottle of liberated German brandy.'

George Stimpson went on to recall the happenings of the following day: 'After pushing towards Bremen and, at one stage, having got patrols actually into the outskirts of the city, 5th Tanks were ordered to break away and motor southwards to meet up with and assist the 53rd Welsh Division, which was heading for Rethem and had for some reason left its own tank support behind. When we arrived at the rendezvous, each squadron was allocated to a different infantry battalion, B Squadron was to support the Monmouthshires, making straight for Rethem, while C Squadron was attached to another battalion which had been ordered first to clear a large wooded area and then make for a village some five miles south of Rethem.

'At the briefing we were told that the infantry had already patrolled into the wood that morning and that it could therefore be considered as being clear of enemy. With this in mind, the first few miles through the wooded area would be carried out at the double, with the infantry riding on the backs of the tanks. The advance was to be along two parallel tracks, with my troop (10 Troop) on the left and Jake's (11 Troop) on the right. At zero hour, both troops advanced along their allotted centre lines and 11 Troop was soon well inside the wood, while 10 Troop, which had more open ground to cross, was still clear of the trees. We suddenly saw a number of friendly fighter aircraft clearly shaping up for an attack with us as their targets, so we took the prudent course of stopping and displaying our recognition panels. 11 Troop, unaware of this delay, continued on into the wood. There was really no reason why they should not have done so, after all, it had already been reported as clear. Eventually they came to a cross-track junction, and slowed down to check the map, when all hell broke loose! They were right in the middle of an ambush with enemy dug in all round the crossing. It was later discovered that the enemy were Marines.

'The last two tanks in the troop managed to pull back and from their reports it soon became clear that a terrific and bloody battle had been fought at the cross-roads, with considerable losses to our side, including Jake's Firefly. It was realised that a full-scale attack would be needed to shift the enemy position. For the time being we halted, but during the night tanks were able to advance down the other track, bypassing the enemy and reaching the village, which was their objective, just before first light.

'As soon as I was able I went to the squadron commander and asked for permission to go back into the wood, to look for the two missing tanks of 10 Troop. This was granted on condition that I took only those members of my own crew who volunteered to come with me. There were no second thoughts given to this and we set off down the road back into the wood. It was rather quiet and frightening, but there were no signs of the enemy and we eventually came to the place where the battle had taken place. The two tanks were still and quiet and there were bodies of British soldiers everywhere. I found Jake's body at the side of his tank, which was in the middle of the cross tracks. He had been killed by machine gun fire.

'I then inspected the tank and found that it had been hit by a bazooka which had struck the armoured cover over the forward extractor fan, just at the side of the driver's head, but had done very little permanent damage to the vehicle. It was obvious, however, that enough chaos and confusion had been created to make the crew think that they had been hit badly and that they must bale out. They were gunned down as they tried to escape.

'It was at this time I took Jake's diary into safe keeping. I was well aware where he had kept it. Later I was able to start the tank and we drove it back to the squadron, where a new crew took it over. Then we continued on to Rethem, where we were to see the slaughter inflicted on the Monmouthshires, who had been sent against a well-defended town with little or no preparation. The town was taken the next day by 10 Troop, who had two commanders acting as infantry and supported by just four tanks. If this was the way the 53rd conducted itself then no wonder it had lost so many men getting nowhere on the way to Arnhem!

'Later, when thinking it all over, I decided that as it was far from certain that I would see the end of the war, the best thing I could do with the diary was to send it home to Jake's mother, and the problem of how to do it was solved when I remembered the "Green Envelope" system* which I used every night for some weeks, sending a few sheets at a time and getting a different young officer to sign the envelopes.'

* The Green Envelope system: soldiers were allowed to send letters home using this system at regular intervals, knowing that the letters would not be subject to the normal unit censorship (although they could still be opened by the base censor). An officer had to sign a statement on the envelope to the effect that the letter contained no classified information.

Appendix A

Soldiers Mentioned in Diary

Arthur	Tpr Arthur *FAIRBURN*. *SQMS* Storeman.
Alf	Tpr Alf *DOLBY*. Great C Sqn character and excellent tank gunner.
Busty	SSM Busty *GREENSLADE*.
Cliff	Sgt Clifford *FISHWICK*. C Squadron. Lost a leg at Villers–Bocage battle in France, 1944.
Claude	L Cpl Claude *COOK*. Big man from Kidderminster. Always smoked a pipe. Tank driver in C Sqn to Sgt E Hartley.
Carlo	Tpr Carlo *CHARLTON*. Big strapping tank gunner.
Dixie	Sgt Dixie *DEAN* (later SSM). Wounded in the desert but rejoined 5 RTR just before it left Home for Italy. Killed near Foggia.
Dusty	Sgt Dusty *RHODES*. C Squadron Fitter Sgt. Killed after war in road accident near Hamm, Germany 1947.
Digger	Sgt Digger *WHITEINLAW*.
Little George (also Stimo)	Sgt George *STIMPSON*. One of Jake's closest friends and a member of the same crew on many occasions. Regular soldier 1938–59, always in C Squadron throughout the war.
George	Tpr George *CARTER*. C Squadron, tank driver. Kept a pet goose at Homs.
Henry	Sgt Henry *HALL*. Military Medal. C Squadron, 11 Troop sergeant.
Jumbo	Sgt Jumbo *HILL*. C Squadron, Tank commander.
Jack	Cpl (later Major, MC) Jack *GARNETT*. Adjutant and OC B Squadron, 5 RTR. First editor of diary.

'Slap Happy' Joe	Sgt Joe LYONS. Member of 5 RTR boxing team pre-war (hence the 'Slap Happy'), brother of Nippy.
'Sure Shot' Jimmy	Tank gunner in C Sqn.
Len	Sgt Len ATKINS. Fitter.
Mad	Tpr Mad COUTTS. Young soldier, spoke good Italian and Arabic. Only had half an ear which he had presumably damaged in a fight. A 'nutcase' but a good soldier.
Middy	Tpr Middy MIDDLETON. Ex-bugler from RTC days in India. Water cart driver, captured just before Knightsbridge, but later escaped and gave useful information on German weapons etc. Killed at Salerno, at same time as Stanley Skeels.
Nippy	Sgt (later SQMS then SSM) Nippy LYONS. Brother of 'Slap Happy' Joe.
Pave	Cpl PAVELY. C Squadron. Killed in desert.
Pooky	Cpl Pooky MINTER. C Squadron fitter. Only 5ft 2in tall.
Ray	Sgt Ray ROGERS. Fitters Sgt.
Red Haggis	Sgt (later Major (QM)) Jock McLEOD. Military Medal winner, Tp Sgt of medium section pre-war at Perham Down. Left 5 RTR early in war (was serving with 1st ARMY in 144 RAC when, as diary explains, they all met him in Tunisia). Became QM 4 RTR after the war.
Snowy	Sgt Snowy HARRIS. C Squadron. Killed in Germany about the same time as Jake. Big blond, six footer.
Stooge	Sgt Stooge ALCOCK. C Squadron, Eccentric, puzzled an MO who saw him baling out and running away from his knocked-out tank using his tin hat to cover his bottom not his head. Great soldier. SSM 'C' Sqn in 1944.
Snake Bite	Tpr Snake Bite THOMSON. C Squadron, tank driver. Ex-circus hand, who was not keen on water as a means of washing, hence the nickname! A fitter.
Stan	Tpr Stanley SKEELS. C Squadron. One of Jake's best friends. Regular soldier and member of 5 RTR pre-war Boxing Team. Killed at Salerno in September '43, crushed to death between two tanks. Difficult man to

	control when he had 'had a few'. Jake's drinking companion. 75mm gunner.
Tweeny	Tpr (later Major (QM)) Dai *MITCHELL*. Regular, 1938 SQMS's driver and member of Rgt Boxing Team pre-war.
Topper	Sgt Topper *BROWN*.
Wag	Sgt Wag *FRY*, eldest of three brothers all RTR. Killed in the desert.
Walter	Cpl Walter *TREADWELL*. Electrician, tall and thin, a very clever electrician.
Woody	Tpr Woody *WOODS*. Radio operator.

Officers Mentioned in Book

Bob Crisp	Major Bob *CRISP* DSO. Famous South African cricketer and journalist. Commanded a squadron in 3 RTR.
Bob	Major (later Lt Col) Bob *MAUNSELL* MC. Regular officer who survived WW2 and later served in 1 RTR in Korea.
Biddy	Major *BIDELL*, commanded 'B' Squadron 5 RTR.
Fearless	Lt Col (later Major Gen) 'Fearless Jim' *HUTTON* CB, CBE, DSO, MC Commanding officer from El Alamein to Tunis. Outstanding CO who was admired by all his men. Later became Director General of Fighting Vehicles at the War Office (1962).
Paddy	Major (later Lt Col) Paddy *DOYLE*, DSO, MC. A 'battle-scarred' 'C' Squadron leader who was Jake's tank commander on numerous occasions (see entry in diary about rescuing him when wounded at El Alamein).
Long Range Mitford	Lt Col (later Brigadier) E.C. *MITFORD*, MC, commanded the 'composite' 5 RTR during the 'Cauldron' battles. Great desert man who helped to build up the Long Range Desert Group.
Steve	Capt *STEVENS*. Tp leader in C Sqn. Killed in desert.
Big Ted	Major *WHITTY*. OC C Squadron for a time, badly wounded in Italy.

Major Ward	Major (later General Sir Richard) *WARD*, GBE, KCB, CB, DSO, MC, a famous RTR soldier who retired after an outstanding military career. Reputed to have had more tanks knocked out under him than anyone else in 5 RTR.
Major Winship	Major H.N. *WINSHIP*. C Sqn leader at the start of the war and commanded 'Z' Sqn in France. A regular soldier since WW1, he had served in India and North West Frontier with RTC armoured car squadrons. Killed in the first action against the Afrika Korps at El Agheila.
Col Willison	Lt Col (later Brigadier) A.C. *WILLISON* was 21C 5 RTR in 1939. Commanded 42 RTR and later 32nd Army Tank Brigade, in Tobruk. Made historic sortie from Tobruk during Op Crusader (flying the same brigade flag which Gen Sir Percy Hobart, who played such a leading part in the development of armoured operations, had flown).

Appendix B

Tank Details

The tanks mentioned in this book cover the early and middle periods of the Second World War starting with the pitifully small numbers of semi-obsolete AFVs with which the British Army had to try to stop the German Panzer divisions in 1940. Thanks to lack of finance between the wars, indifference, opposition, and a sharp conflict over what was the best role for the tank, Great Britain lost the commanding lead in tank prowess which she had held at the end of the First World War. So the German *Blitzkrieg* was met by a handful of British tanks, for the most part out-gunned, under-armoured and mechanically unreliable. The problem was compounded by the loss of much precious equipment at Dunkirk, which meant that we simply had to go on producing what we could, instead of being able to make improvements which would have interfered with the few production lines available. This state of affairs was not rectified until the enormous potential of American industry was harnessed to war production.

In 1939/40 the USA had even fewer tanks than Britain, but the Americans were so alarmed by the success of the Germans in Europe that they rapidly put their technical prowess (and more importantly, their 'get up and go!') into producing tanks and other armoured fighting vehicles. By the end of the war they had built a staggering 88,276 tanks and a grand total of 337,000 AFVs. First to gain the benefit of this product were not American tank battalions, but rather the British forces in the Western Desert. Jake tells of the introduction of the Stuart light tanks – called Honeys by the British crews, which clearly shows how much they liked them. These were followed by the first of the medium tanks, the M3 Grant, with its powerful 75mm gun in a cumbersome side turret. Despite the awkwardness of this ad hoc arrangement, the gun did help to redress some of the balance and caused Rommel some severe shocks. As well as being able to engage enemy tanks with some chance of penetration, it could also fire HE ammunition and was thus able to deal with anti-tank guncrews. This was a facility which had been lacking on British tanks ever since the end of the First World War! The Grant was soon replaced, at least in part, by the ubiquitous Sherman, in time for Montgomery's offensive at El Alamein. Undoubtedly the Sherman was one of the greatest tanks of WW2, and saw service all over the world. Nearly 50,000 Shermans of all types were built in the USA, there being many derivatives, specialised vehicles on the Sherman chassis, etc. Jake's last tank was one of these, being an upgunned Sherman, known as a Firefly. This was a British attempt to get on equal terms with the German Tigers and Panthers, by mounting a hard-hitting 17-pounder gun into a Sherman M4.

Below are shown details of the tanks in which Jake served.

1. MARK III MEDIUM
    1926 : 13½ tons : 5 Crew
    Overall dimensions: Height 9ft 10½in : Width 9ft 1½in : Length 17ft 6in
    Armament: Main: 1 × 3 pdr. Secondary: 3 × .303in Vickers MG (1 coax 2 in hull)
    Engine: Armstrong Siddeley 90bhp . 16mph*. 120mls
    Armour Thickness: 8–12mm
    Remarks:
    Standard tank of RTC during interwar years. It was of riveted construction and was first British tank with all round traversing turret. Although a small number were used in North Africa, their main use was for training.

2. MARK VI LIGHT
    1938 : 5½ tons : 3 Crew
    Overall dimensions: Height 7ft 3½in : Width 6ft 9in : Length 13ft
    Armament: Main 1 × .5in Vickers MG (MK VIC had 1 × 15mm MG and 1 × 7.92mm MG instead). Secondary: 1 × .303in Vickers

* The speed given throughout the Appendix is maximum road speed, and the following mileage figure indicates endurance.

Engine: Meadows 89bhp . 35mph . 130mls
Armour Thickness: 4–14mm
Remarks:
Bulk of British tank strength in 1940 was made up of MK VI light tanks. They were used in France and Middle East in 1940–41. Developed from Carden–Lloyd series of light tanks and carriers.

3. MARK I CRUISER (A9)
    1938 : 12 tons : 6 Crew
    Overall Dimensions: Height 8ft 4in : Width 8ft 4in : Length 19ft 3in
    Armament: Main: 1 × 2 pdr. (Close Support version had 3.7 in mortar.)
    Secondary: 3 × .303in Vickers MGs (1 coax 2 in aux turrets)
    Engine: AEC 6 cylinder 150bhp . 25mph . 100mls
    Armour Thickness: 6–14mm
    Remarks:
    First example of the demand for fast, handy tanks to be used for the mobile battle (they were called 'Cruisers'); saw action in France and the Western Desert.

4. MARK II CRUISER (A10)
    1939 : 13¾ tons : 4 Crew
    Overall Dimensions: Height 8ft 6in : Width 8ft 3½in : Length 18ft 1in
    Armament: Main: 1 × 2 pdr. (CS version had 3.7in mortar.)
    Secondary: 1 × .303in Vickers MG (coax)
    Engine: AEC 6 cylinder 150bhp . 16mph . 100mls
    Armour Thickness: 30mm
    Remarks:
    More heavily armoured version of A9 saw action as for A9. Orders were restricted as it was decided to concentrate on a new type of cruiser with a Christie suspension. MK IIA had 2x Besa MGs and crew of 5.

5. INFANTRY MARK II MATILDA (A12)
    1939 : 26½ tons : 4 Crew
    Overall Dimensions: Height 8ft : Width 8ft 6in : Length 18ft 5in
    Armament: Main: 1 × 2 pdr. (CS version had 3 in how)
    Secondary: 1 × .303 Vickers MG (coax) or 7.92mm Besa MG
    Engine: AEC 2 × 87bhp . 15mph . 70mls

Armour Thickness: 20–78mm

Remarks:

There were five marks of Matilda II which differed mainly in engine. Heavily armoured the I tank was primarily for infantry support. 5 RTR only had them for a short period in June 1941, during the Battleaxe offensive, when they were hastily equipped with tanks belonging to 44 RTR (the tanks having arrived on the *Tiger* convoy ahead of the Regiment), entrained for Mersa Matruh on 16 June and thence to leaguer NE of Charing Cross. They did not however take part in any fighting and 10 days later 44 RTR arrived to take over their tanks while the Fifth went back to Beni Yusef to draw up Honeys.

6.   MARK III CRUISER (A13)

1939 : 14¾ tons : 4 Crew

Overall Dimensions: Height 8ft 6in : Width 8ft 4in : Length 19ft 9in

Armament: Main: 1 × 2 pdr. Secondary: 1 × .303in Vickers MG (coax)

Engine: Nuffield Liberty I 340bhp . 30mph . 90mls

Armour Thickness: 6–14mm

Remarks:

First Cruiser with Christie suspension. MKs IV and IVA were almost identical, main difference being an increase to 30mm max armour protection of turret and frontal plating of hull.

7.   MARK VI CRUISER (A15) CRUSADER

1941 : 19 tons (Crusader III was ¾ ton heavier) : 5–3 Crew

Overall Dimensions: Height 7ft 4in : Width 8ft 8in : Length 19ft 8in

Armament: Main: 1 × 2 pdr. (1 × 6 pdr. on Crusader III)

Secondary: 2 × 7.92m Besa (one coax, one in aux turret.)

Engine: Nuffield Liberty II/III/IV 340bhp . 26–27mph . 100mls

Armour Thickness: 7–40mm (7–52mm Crusader III)

Remarks:

CS tank had 3 in howitzer instead of 2 pdr. Removal of auxiliary turret gave more storage space and reduced crew to 4 in Crusader II and 3 in Crusader III.

8.   STUART I (LIGHT TANK M3) (HONEY)

1941 : 12½ tons : 4 Crew

Overall Dimensions: Height 8ft 3in : Width 7ft 4in : Length 14ft 11in

Armament: Main: 1 × 37mm Secondary: 2 × .30 Browning MG (1 coax)
Engine: Continental 7 cyl radial 250bhp . 36mph . 70mls
Armour Thickness: 12–38mm
Remarks:
Nicknamed the 'Honey' by the British who liked the reliability and
robustness of this American light tank, despite the fact that it was
still under-armoured and under-gunned.

9. GRANT I (MEDIUM TANK M3)
    1942 : 28½ tons : 6 Crew
    Overall Dimensions: Height 9ft 4in : Width 9ft : Length 18ft 7 in
    Armament: Main: 1 × 75mm (in hull) 1 × 37mm (in turret)
    Secondary: 1 × .30 Browning MG (coax)
    Engine: Continental 9 cyl radial 340bhp . 26mph . 144mls
    Armour Thickness: 13–57mm
    Remarks:
    First of the American medium tanks to enter British service. The
    Grant's 75mm gun with its dual capability – so that it could fire HE
    as well as AP – came as a considerable shock to the Germans.

10. SHERMAN I & II (MEDIUM TANK M4)
    1942 : 30 tons : 5 Crew
    Overall Dimensions: Height 10ft 4in : Width 8ft 9in : Length 20ft 4in
    Armament: Main: 1 × 75mm Secondary 2 × .30 Browning MG
    (1 coax)
    Engine: Continental 9 cyl radial 400bhp . 24mph . 85mls
    Armour Thickness: 12–76mm
    Remarks:
    Probably the most widely used tank of WW2. Crews liked its
    reliability, but did not like the way it 'brewed up' quickly when hit
    (some called it the 'Ronson Lighter'). More Shermans were produced
    than any other tank.

11. SHERMAN VC FIREFLY
    1944 : 32 tons : 4 Crew
    Overall Dimensions: Height 9ft : Width 8ft 9in : Length 25ft 9in
    Armament: Main: 1 × 17 pdr. Secondary: 1 × .30 Browning MG
    coax

1 × .50 Browning in AA Mtg
Engine: Chrysler A57 425bhp . 25mph . 100mls
Armour Thickness: 25–90 tons
Remarks:
This was a British attempt to up-gun the Sherman. It was normally issued on a scale of one per troop in an armoured regiment from February 1944 onwards.

Notes

Chapter One

1. It was fitting for a Glaswegian like Jake to leave the UK via the Clyde. As he was a tank driver he travelled aboard the *Clan Chattan*, which carried the Regiment's vehicles, while the bulk of 5RTR soldiers sailed on the *Stirling Castle* which left Liverpool on 1 November 1940. The route was around South Africa, in order to avoid running the gauntlet through the Mediterranean which would have saved some forty days, but since the Luftwaffe had air superiority over the Med at that time, it was far too great a risk to take. The *Clan Chattan* was bombed and sunk off Crete on 14 February 1942.
2. 20 November is the anniversary of the Battle of Cambrai (1917), when tanks were first used successfully and in sufficient numbers to make a considerable impact on the battle. Ever since it has been kept as the RTR Regimental Day, so it was fitting that they could combine 'Crossing the Line' ceremonies with their Cambrai Day celebrations.
3. 'The Blue' was the name which the soldiers used for the Western Desert. Men would speak of 'going up the Blue', when they meant they were going into the desert.
4. C Squadron RTR was heavily involved in the Agedabia battle. They had been ordered back from El Agheila on 2 April when Rommel attacked, and the Regiment had withdrawn, using drills which it had long practised on Salisbury Plain – one squadron acting as rearguard and then leap-frogging through another which had taken up defensive positions on the next feature to the rear and so on. They were pursued by a 'cloud of dust' which, as it came closer, could be seen to contain tanks and vehicles – a force of considerable size. C Squadron were rearguard at the time and let the enemy come on until they were well

inside the effective range of the 2-pounder gun (under 1,000 yards). George Stimpson recalls: '. . . when the firing began it was carried out in the well-practised manner of a hull-down shoot – fire three rounds, reverse a little and come up in a slightly different position, then three more rounds and so on. This had been instilled into us from our earliest training days and we scored countless hits without one of our tanks being damaged – undoubtedly this was the way to fight a tank v tank battle . . . After what was really a brief encounter the squadron was ordered to disengage and rejoin the regiment. This was no problem as most of us were in good hull-down positions, but just as we started pulling back some other tanks appeared, went forward over the ridge and charged the enemy, losing five tanks complete with crews – very heroic but definitely NOT the way to do it. History has shown that if anyone learned from this action, it was Rommel!'

5. Liddell Hart says of this action in *The Tanks*: '. . . All four tanks were knocked out, but by their sacrifice they enabled the column to get safely away down the road to Tobruk, besides knocking out an estimated total of eleven German armoured cars and three anti-tank guns.'

6. The brigade was in fact commanded by Brigadier Alec Gatehouse who had commanded 4RTR in France and who went on to command the newly formed 10th Armoured Division. While it was forming he was switched to command 1st Armoured Division when General Lumsden was wounded, thus becoming the first RTR officer to command an armoured division in battle, but he was himself wounded soon after the battle began.

Chapter Two

1. This method of defence, which is known as the box leaguer, is still used by armoured formations in similar circumstances. The formation is adopted for administrative convenience as well as defence. It was standard practice for the British to withdraw a few miles after a battle, before forming a leaguer, while the Germans tended to leaguer at dusk exactly where they had finished the day's fighting. This gave the enemy a much better chance of recovering damaged equipment and for destroying that of the enemy they found on the battlefield. However, they were much more vulnerable to attack. Undoubtedly the

most difficult and dangerous job at night was undertaken by the resupply echelon, which had to find the unit leaguer in the dark, bring up fuel, ammunition and rations, with little more than a six-figure map reference to go on – and the maps were notoriously inaccurate! The Germans favoured a policy of firing flares to illuminate their leaguers as they reckoned this made them easier to protect, but the British normally preferred as little noise and as few lights as possible.

2. How many tank crewmen will remember nights spent like this? The tank bivouac was an excellent affair, made of stout canvas, which fitted to the side of the tank but it did take time to put up and take down and might have to be left *in situ* if the leaguer were suddenly attacked and the tanks had to move out in a hurry.

3. It is interesting to see how much the opposing armies liked each other's rations. For example bully beef, that scourge of the British Tommy, was considered something of a delicacy by the DAK, while the German equivalent (tins were stamped AM and were known as '*Altermann*' (Old Man) or Asinius Mussolini ('Mussolini's Backside')) were eaten with relish by our soldiers. Lime juice was a very sensible issue in the desert, to make up for the lack of fresh fruit.

4. This refers of course to the Brigade Group principle, where the brigade commander had under his command a mixed force of all arms – tanks, infantry, artillery, engineers, plus the supporting A and Q Services, so that his group was virtually self-contained.

Chapter Three

1. See Appendix B for a description of the Grant tank. The first ten Grants arrived in 5RTR on 29 January, and by the end of February the regiment had eighteen Stuarts and twenty Grants.

2. 1RB were what was termed a 'motor battalion'. They were mounted in lorries' half-tracks and worked very closely with the tanks they supported, a motor rifle company normally being allocated to each armoured regiment.

3. Jock Campbell was not killed in battle, but as the result of a motoring accident. He was travelling in his staff car near Halfaya Pass in February 1942, when it skidded on the slippery clay road and overturned. At the time it was being driven by his ADC, Roy Farran, later to achieve great things himself in the field of unconventional

warfare. In his book *Winged Dagger* (Collins, 1948) Farran graphically describes how he was thrown out and knocked unconscious by the crash, coming to and finding the General dead on the sand beside him: '. . . The country all round was deserted and I contemplated suicide. How could I face the world with the knowledge that I had killed the greatest man in the desert in his hour of triumph?'

4. The Arabs who live in the desert say that after five days of the *Khamseen* even murder can be excused!

5. The Grants were certainly quite a shock to the Germans, causing Rommel to write in his journal: 'The advent of the new American tank had torn great holes in our tanks. Our entire force now stood in heavy and destructive combat with a superior enemy.'

6. Probably the most feared weapon in the Afrika Korps arsenal was the 88 mm Flak 18. Accurate as a sniper's rifle, the 88 mm in the anti-tank role could easily score a kill at 4,500 yards. It had a 21 lb AP shell which would penetrate 105 mm of steel plate at 1,000 yards and 30°. The British had an equally potent anti-tank weapon in their 3.7 in AA gun, but this was never used in the anti-tank role except in emergencies. It could be argued that Rommel hastened his own defeat by the removal of these AA guns for use in the anti-tank role, thus leaving his precious supply bases all the more vulnerable to Allied aircraft.

Chapter Four

1. 7th Armoured Division had once again been reorganised: this time the armoured division took the place of the brigade group as the basic battle formation. Armoured brigade groups were redesignated as armoured brigades, the gunners and sappers returned to under divisional control and the armoured brigade was balanced by an infantry brigade of three battalions of lorried infantry. This basic organisation of two brigades, one armoured and one infantry, would remain the 'norm' for the armoured division for the rest of the war, while the regiments in 7th Armoured Division returned to the UK from Italy at the end of 1943. This continuity meant that everyone got used to working together and was one of the major reasons for the division's continued run of success in battle.

2. Radio communications are the lifeblood of any armoured formation, but without strict wireless discipline (e.g. the proper use of radio

procedure, codes, etc) the whole thing can quickly become unworkable even on the smallest net. When one remembers that there would be at least sixty to seventy wireless sets in an armoured regiment at that time, then strict discipline was clearly essential. The difficulties of running such a net were outweighed by the tremendous advantages gained, the most obvious ones being that everyone in the regiment knew *exactly* what was happening in any part of their battle area, and that the CO could listen and speak to any one of his tank commanders if he wished to do so. This made for the speedy passage of information.

3. Jake is probably referring here to the Anti-Mine Roller Attachment (AMRA) which was fitted to the Matilda and Valentine tanks. This consisted of a number of heavy rollers on a frame which was pushed in front of the tank and detonated the mines by pressure. Small numbers were in service in the Middle East, some fitted with 'Carrot' which was a demolition charge of some 600 lb of HE, designed for blowing gaps in obstacles. Most of the lanes cleared mechanically at El Alamein were cleared by the Scorpion Flail tank – 32 Scorpion-fitted Matildas being used at Alamein, with mixed success, so most of the gapping had to be done by sappers prodding for mines by hand – a slow and hazardous business.

4. George Stimpson, who was also in Doyle's crew as 37 mm gunner, vividly remembered the incident: 'The bridgehead was very crowded with infantry trying to dig into the rock-hard ground and tanks milling around, but for a time little action and no enemy tanks in sight . . . we were being shelled quite heavily with airbursting shells, which could not do a lot of damage to a tank provided the cupola lid was closed and there was always a temptation to open up and of course observation was so much better . . . also the major had a squadron to control and that forced him to continually open up for a few minutes at a time when he put on his steel helmet and had a good look round. We made a point of reminding him . . . but eventually he said, "Bugger it, I'll stick to my beret."

'He had hardly finished saying it when a shell exploded overhead and he was hit on the head by shrapnel which knocked him out stone cold and he fell between the turret basket and the hull of the tank. I managed to bandage his head with a towel and when he came to he wanted to get out of the tank so Jake got out and went to the side door, where we pushed the Major to him. I then got out . . . we soon realised that we had done a bloody stupid thing, although we were able to find some cover in a shallow gun pit . . . but there was still no cover from airbursts; however, we were able to give the Major some better first aid treatment. After this Jake made it clear that, like it or not, we were going back into the tank and signalled to the rest of the crew to open the side door, Major Paddy went in a lot quicker than he came out . . .'

5. 'Marble Arch' had been erected by the Italians before the war at the halfway point on the coastal road between Egypt and Tripoli.

Chapter Five

1. The British 6-pounder anti-tank gun had an armour penetration of 2.7 in at 1,000 yds, and was brought in to replace the ineffective 2-pounder gun which had a maximum effective range of only 600 yds and was very difficult to conceal. However, the advent of the Tiger, whose frontal armour it could not penetrate, led to the 6-pounder being replaced by the 17-pounder in Royal Artillery anti-tank batteries, and it was passed on down to infantry battalions. It was in one of these infantry anti-tank gun platoons that the gun notched up such an impressive 'bag' during the Battle of Medenine.

2. *Fascines.* The big bundles of sticks are called 'fascines' and have long been a recognised way of getting armoured vehicles across minor obstacles which do not need to be bridged, thus saving precious tank bridges for the wider and more tricky gaps.

3. *Moaning Minnies.* The 15cm Nebelwerfer 41 first appeared in 1941 and went into large-scale action in 1942. It was a simple six-barrelled field artillery rocket launcher, the rockets being fired singly at two-second intervals by one of the four-man crew using a small electrical generator. The rockets made a very distinctive noise in flight, hence their name, 'Moaning Minnies'. As the photograph shows, they were mounted on a two-wheeled carriage and were usually towed by an SdKfz 11/1 tractor.

4. *The Tiger.* Panzerkampfwagen VI Ausf E (SdKfz 181), or just plain 'Tiger' as it was usually called, was one of the best tanks of the war. Its 88 mm KwK 36 gun was from the same basic design as the 88 mm Flak 18 and 36, and had an equally outstanding performance. The British first had to face the Tiger in Tunisia, but it had already been in action in Russia. With a battle weight of 56 tons and a crew of 5 it

was a formidable opponent. Probably the most famous engagement ever carried out by a Tiger against British troops was the occasion when Obersturmführer – SS Michael Wittmann and his Tiger tank held up the *entire* British 7th Armoured Division at Hill 213 on the road from Villers–Bocage in Normandy, knocking out 25 vehicles to add to his already amazing score of 119 Soviet tanks knocked out in Russia! Tiger 2, Koenigstiger, was an even more formidable opponent. At a battle weight of 68 tons its 21 ft long 88 mm KwK 43 L/71 gun eliminated all would-be opponents with ease. Fortunately only a few Tiger 2s were ever produced!

Chapter Six

1. Long Range Desert Group. The LRDG was a force raised by Major R.A. Bagnold in 1940 for long range reconnaissance behind enemy lines, to which later was added a strike element as conceived by David Stirling (it became the forerunner of the Special Air Service). They inflicted considerable damage and destruction on such targets as enemy airfields.

Chapter Seven

1. *Ramadan*, the ninth month of the Mohammedan year, which is the Moslem Lent or holy month, during which true believers will both fast and abstain from drinking during daylight hours – to include even not swallowing their own spittle in extreme cases.
2. LST = Landing Ship Tank.
3. The capture of Cardito was considered by the Rifle Brigade, whom IRTR were supporting, as their most successful action in Italy. The village was some 700 yards long and very straggly: '. . . quite a task for a motor company which had only two platoons and only assaulted about forty strong.' Despite this, the attack on its narrow front against considerable opposition was completely successful.
4. This refers to an article which appeared in *Picture Post* magazine on 27 June 1942, entitled 'A General Grant arrives in Libya'. Snowy Harris was featured on the front cover, posed in his tank turret, and clearly had his leg pulled thereafter! He was killed in Germany towards the end of the war.

5a. Half-track Whites. These were American in origin but also built in the UK and USSR. They were one of the most useful and widely used vehicles of the war (over 40,000 produced). They weighed about 9½ tons, could carry ten or twelve passengers in addition to a crew of three, had a top speed on roads of 40–45 mph, and a range of 180–213 miles. They were lightly armoured, and usually had a canvas top to the passenger compartment. They were also used to carry anti-tank guns, mortars, artillery pieces, etc.

5b. M10 tank destroyer. Based on the standard Sherman M4 chassis and engine, but with a much lighter armoured open-topped turret, the M10 (called the Wolverine) mounted a 3-inch gun. Most of those in British service were converted into the Achilles tank destroyer, by substituting a British 17-pounder for the 3-inch gun. Max speed was 30 mph and range 200 miles.

Bibliography

Liddell Hart, B.H.: *The Tanks*, published by Cassell
Liddell Hart, B.H. (ed): *The Rommel Papers*, Collins
Montgomery, Field Marshal B.: *Memoirs*, Collins

Picture Post Vol. 15, 27 June 1942, Hulton
The TANK Magazine Vol. 159, No. 680, July 1977, RHQ RTR
5RTR War Diary 1938–45
5RTR Battle Drill issues for November 1942 and June 1943 (amended
  November 1943)

Index

TANKS, MILITARY FORMATIONS AND UNITS